FOREWORD BY JACK L. STOTTS

Sermons for the City

FOURTH PRESBYTERIAN CHURCH
CHICAGO, ILLINOIS

Elam Davies and John M. Buchanan

PROVIDENCE HOUSE PUBLISHERS
Franklin, Tennessee

Library of Congress Catalog Card Number: 96-69158

ISBN: 1-57736-008-7

Scripture quotations used in this book come from the following sources:

Revised Standard Version of the Bible. Copyright
1946, 1952 Division of Christian Education of the
National Council of the Churches of Christ in the
United States of America. Used by permission.

New Revised Standard Version Bible. Copyright 1989
Division of Christian Education of the National
Council of the Churches of Christ in the United States
of America. Used by permission.

Cover photograph by Micah Marty. Used by permission.

Cover by Bozeman Design

Book coordinated by Louise D. Howe

Published by
PROVIDENCE HOUSE PUBLISHERS
238 Seaboard Lane • Franklin, Tennessee 37067
800-321-5692

Contents

Foreword

SERMONS FOR THE CITY. THERE IS A TOUCH OF ARROGANCE in the use of *the* here. The sermons included in this collection were preached in a city—Chicago. But the particularity of that location encompasses issues and concerns that apply to all cities, as well as suburbs, smaller cities, and towns. To address the immediate and the specific with the universal good news will always be locale-specific, while simultaneously breaking constricting boundaries of any parochialism or imperialism of place.

These sermons were also preached to a particular congregation and will bear, as they should, the marks of the congregation's life. Fourth Presbyterian Church, Chicago, has an enduring history of preachers who have addressed with great power a gathered people. Their individual and corporate ministry and witness to Jesus Christ have been sculpted by that proclaimed word. But the people have also provided an environment of expectations and openness that enables and empowers strong preaching. For it is in the transaction of people and preacher that the word comes alive. As one "hears" these sermons through his or her eyes, each reader should locate them initially at least in their context: A preacher stands before a congregation which fills a cathedral-like sanctuary. Looking out on some, down on others, up at a few, the preacher cannot fail to hear the honking of taxicabs scurrying to beat the lights before they turn red. The world intrudes on the sanctuary, as it should, reminding people and preacher that the word pro-claimed and heard today is for the whole world, not just for those gathered together for an hour of worship.

Many in that congregation—as in others throughout the land—take the preacher and the sermon for granted, a given which does not require reflection. Preaching for such hearers is simply "there," to be received with gratitude and appreciation, or dismissed as "not quite up to par." For most people, preaching is not a topic for analysis or reflection.

Yet preaching is a subject in itself, worthy of our thought. How shall we understand this activity? Preaching is, first, a gift of God for us and for all, but it is also a task to be undertaken.

Though preaching is a gift, I want first to affirm that it is a task. Indeed, it is a relentless master. To be frank, it is hard work.

For example, what other medium of communication requires such multiple talents? One must be a researcher as diligent as Einstein, surveying the universe of the Scriptures—their context, their content—wrestling with the words to find the Word, yet knowing that that wrestling is dependent on God's Spirit opening up the Word.

And one must be an author. Whether one outlines what is to be said on paper or scripts it in one's mind, one must be a skilled writer to shape a word that can be heard.

And one must be as an actor or actress, delivering the lines one has written, but self-directed, with no coaching, no dress rehearsals for last-minute corrections. It is hard work. And it is hard work because of those to whom one speaks.

For one must take the research and the script and mount a pulpit and gaze down and out at a crowd populated with as many expectations and needs as there are occupied pews. Some of those people the preacher knows. There, over there, in the third pew right, is a man just widowed, constricted by a straitjacket of grief.

There, over there, in the tenth pew, left, is the radiant couple just married, for whom the world is open and saturated with joy.

Way in the back is the woman who has too much of the world's
goods and sits far from the pulpit for fear that if she gets too close,
God will get too close to her, and she will then be tempted to sell
all that she has and give it to the poor. About midway back
crouches the man in a seemingly robust body diagnosed just
Friday as having inoperable cancer. Meanwhile, up in the balcony
there is that disheveled, dirty, hungry, and homeless man again,
seeking a home for his heart.

And there, right there in front of you, is the familiar figure
with the folded arms and chiseled face; it is the resident Doubting
Thomas, daring you to say anything he cannot refute, yet
maybe hoping you will. And even worse, you know that lurking
somewhere in the congregation—every congregation—is the
seventh-grade English teacher waiting to pounce when you end a
sentence with a preposition. And even a Welsh accent cannot
prevail over such an egregious error!

But there they all are—the young and the old and those in
between, the strangers and the friends, the visitors and the old-
timers, the ill and the healthy, the alert and the sleepy, those
hungry for a word, and others who, though always present, have
forgotten or choose to ignore that there can be a fresh word.

And there the preacher stands—a flimsy few pages of text in
hand. Not the masterpiece he had intended. For he had been interrupted by the call to visit ninety-year-old Dorothy Smith, admitted
for her last visit to the hospital, awaiting the hearing of the
Twenty-third Psalm one last time.

And there the preacher stands—looking out at people who
look up and are eager to be fed. No wonder the preacher prays
before beginning.

Preaching is hard work. But preaching is a work that also
keeps one humble. The better the preacher the greater the temptation, because the preacher knows that preaching's effectiveness
finally depends upon the Spirit of God. That Spirit takes frail
human words and converts these human vessels into carriers of
the divine. And the preacher knows better than any that the Word
is proclaimed, when it is authentically proclaimed, for the good of
the neighbor and to the glory of God. The preacher knows that the
sermon can be both a stunning performance and an absolute

failure if it focuses attention on the preacher personally or on the artistry of the sermon. For the preacher and the preacher's sermon succeed when the hearers' hearts, minds, and wills are firmly clamped onto the reality of God's presence and power. The sermon is a "success" not when the preacher is applauded but when the church is built up, and people are helped along the way.

And preaching is hard work because it is so relentless—Sunday, after Sunday, after Sunday. Mike Nichols, the well-known and acclaimed director of movies and stage plays, recounts that there was only one time that he was ever cruel to an actor. The year was 1976. The play was *Streamers*, which he directed. The actor had been playing his role for three months, and Nichols came by to take another look. He said to the actor: "It was all beautiful, poetical, mechanical. Listen, what do you think your job is? To learn the words? The usher can do that. Your job is the say them for the first time every time. To say the words for the first time. Every time."

This account challenges all who mount the pulpit Sunday after Sunday, year after year. The constant danger, the threat, the possibility for those of us whose vocation is to deal with words is to let the words be poetic, beautiful, but mechanical. Then they will be drained of life, reduced to insignificance by repetition. Then we let routine centrifuge out of our words the wonder, excitement, and life-giving power of the Word. Then we allow our weariness or laziness to drive out the vital, first-time quality of the word of God's love in Jesus Christ.

This preaching that is God's gift is not only glorious but hard work. It is hard in another sense. It is a hard word. It is a hard word to say, at least initially, because people do not want to hear words of judgment.

During the drafting of "A Brief Statement of Faith" for the Presbyterian Church (U.S.A.), the committee responsible sent out to the whole of the denomination a draft proposal for consideration and response. We received an overwhelming response from over seventeen thousand persons or groups. One line in particular was a focal point for disagreement. It was the one that confessed, "We deserve God's condemnation."

The majority of respondents found this sentence to be unacceptable, too harsh, too guilt-producing. Two suggested changes that reflected many other opinions were these: "Why don't you say, 'Some people' deserve God's condemnation?" The second was surely from a school teacher. It read: "Why don't you say, 'We deserve God's evaluation?'" Happily, the General Assembly confirmed the original proposal.

We live—perhaps all people have—but we live in a time when people are hungry for words that caress, not challenge, for words that are pleasant, not harsh. "Successful" preaching is often associated with words that confirm what we want to hear, that soothe troubled spirits without troubling contented minds. H. Richard Niebuhr, over sixty years ago, characterized easy religion in this way: "A god without wrath brought men without sin into a kingdom without judgment through the ministrations of a Christ without a cross" (*The Kingdom of God in America*, [Willett, Clark and Co., 1937], 193).

Yet there is no preaching without the proclamation of the Cross. The Cross is the sign of God's judgment upon our waywardness, the call to recognize that none of us is as good as we think we are and that all of us participate in the crucifixion of Christ. The Cross is a sign that both religion and empire go wrong, and both are always less righteous than they pretend to be. That can be a hard word, and people can turn away, like the rich young ruler whom Jesus rebuked for making wealth his god, or Israel, which forgot its God. Preaching is a hard word.

But the paradox is this: Without the Cross at the center of preaching, there is no healing balm. For the preaching of the Cross and the suffering of God's Christ are the proclamation of the God with holes in his hands. And without that depth of suffering, we cannot proclaim or claim the God who knows our suffering, our pain, our loss, our grief, our sorrows.

Peter De Vries was a novelist who combined a Reformed theology with a sense of the comedic. In one of his novels, *The Blood of the Lamb* (Little, Brown, 1961), the comedic is not lost but subordinated to the tragic.

De Vries tells the story of Don Wanderhope, twice widowed, whose delight and joy of his life was his young daughter Carol. She was diagnosed with leukemia that went into a state of remission, allowing her to return home from the hospital. But the relief was not for long. Soon Carol was back in the hospital bed.

One day, in desperation, Wanderhope stopped in a Roman Catholic church on the way to the hospital. There he prayed before the shrine of St. Jude, the patron of lost and hopeless causes. For a time it appeared that either or both medical or divine powers could be trusted as Carol responded to an experimental drug.

Buoyed by her progress, Wanderhope was merrily on the way to the hospital with a birthday cake in hand. He stopped again at the church to say a word of thanks. His prayer was interrupted by a night nurse from the hospital who urged him to go quickly to Carol's bedside. An infection had set in. Medicine and religion had both betrayed his hopes.

> He knew it was time to say good-by. He whispered to Carol, "The Lord bless thee and keep thee. The Lord make his face shine upon thee, and be gracious to thee. The Lord lift up his countenance upon thee, and give thee peace." A little while later Carol died. Wanderhope retreated to the bar down the street and drank until the bartender refused to serve him any more.
>
> When he left the bar, he passed the church of St. Catherine. He remembered that he had left the birthday cake inside in his haste to get to the hospital that morning. He went inside and found the cake in the pew where he had left it. He took it outside, turned to look up at the crucified Christ hanging over the doorway of the church. Suddenly he vented his rage and despair.
>
> "I took the cake out of the box and balanced it a moment on the palm of my hand. . . . Then my arm drew back and let fly with all the strength within me. . . . It was miracle enough that the pastry should reach its target at all, at that height from the sidewalk. The more so that it should land squarely, just beneath the crown of thorns. Then through scalded eyes I seemed to see the hands free themselves of the nails and move slowly toward the soiled face. Very slowly, very deliberately, with infinite patience, the icing was wiped from the eyes and flung away. I could see it fall in clumps to the porch steps. Then the cheeks were wiped down with the same sense of grave and gentle ritual, with all the kind sobriety of one whose voice could be heard saying, 'Suffer the little children to come unto me. . . . For of such is the kingdom of heaven.'"

Thus Wanderhope found himself at the foot of the cross, bearing true and faithful witness to his loss and to his rage, and encountered there one who like a clown shared the sadness in the ritual of wiping pastry from his face. It was not much consolation, but it did suggest a transcendent throb of compassion. It enabled him to carry on, still grieving, but at least it was an alternative to the muzzle of a gun. (Qtd. by Allen D. Verhey, Institute of Religion, *New Horizons*, Winter/Spring 1994, 22:2. Used by permission.)

Preaching the Cross reveals judgment upon our lives personally and socially. But there is as well the sign of hope, the throb of compassion at the heart of the universe. There is the reminder in the preaching of the Cross that there is no Easter without Good Friday, no victory without defeat, no fullness of life without repentance, no church of Jesus Christ without the proclamation of the Cross.

But the cross is the Cross of Jesus Christ. So it is the good news of God's love that preaching brings to the church and to the world. It is God's yes that follows God's no. This preaching is the way of expanding our little worlds into vaster ones, of calling us to attend to the life beyond the commonplace, to a city more inclusive than our restrictive neighborhoods, to the light that shines in the darkness.

David Douglas, in a meditative book entitled *Wilderness Sojourn* [Harper & Row, 1987], describes setting up camp as dusk descends upon the desert: "But to enter the wilderness invariably accompanied by others can be like camping at dusk with a lantern. Comfort and security are provided, but the surroundings are kept well at bay. We are turned inward, enclosed in a tight circle of light. Only if we momentarily relinquish the lantern does the night begin to appear with stars and shapes and silhouettes, stretching out limitlessly with unnerving beauty" (p. 11).

It is not that what we enjoy and appreciate and give is not good. It is. It is that it is not good enough—not good enough for those of us called to be followers of the God of the universe, brothers and sisters of all people and of creatures great and small. It is not enough to love our little private worlds when there is a whole world to be embraced. And preaching points us to the light and invites us to point others to the light—a light that overcomes the darkness. And preaching the Cross affirms God's presence with us in our suffering and loss and need.

I remember with great appreciation Elam Davies making this point in the last sermon preached at Fourth Presbyterian Church before his retirement. In his engaging, dramatic style, he held us as in a spell as he told of an experience he and his wife Grace shared at the Great Orme, in Wales—a place where people came to see the sunset over the ocean, spraying an array of colors in the heavens which was reflected and magnified in the waters, God's pyrotechnical display, he said.

He and Grace, Elam reported, were parked where they could observe the view. Elam said he saw a ramshackle car drive up next to them—more ramshackle even than theirs. He looked ever so discreetly into the car, and this is what he saw.

An older couple in the front seat got out, went to the back doors of the car, opened them, and helped to a seated position their son who had been struck by a very incapacitating condition. He could not move of his own accord. His father and mother tugged him up so that he was now sitting, looking forward. And just as the sunset was at the height of its magnificence, they put their fingers under his chin and lifted his head so he could see the beauty.

Elam said: "I knew at that moment that God can dazzle us with all the magnificence of the universe. But the secret of the universe is not finally in the beauty of the universe. The secret of the universe is the love that comes to us despite our frailty and in our need. The heart of the universe reveals its glory in the compassion, grace, and love that come when we need them most, in a mother and father lifting up the son's head so that he could see the glorious light."

And Elam concluded: "There it is. There it is. And there you are, my boy, you matter to parents, to God, and to all of us who confess the crucified Christ as Lord." So there it is: without the Cross of judgment and of suffering love, there is no good news of God's love of such, and of God's presence with us in our need.

Preaching is God's gift to the church, for the church, and for the world. It is a strange and arduous task. It is a humble endeavor beside other forms of public communication. But it is the carrier of what must be heard if anything is heard—the Word of God which calls us into new life, a life where in giving we find fulfillment.

And preaching goes on and on and on and on. Preachers come and go. But the preaching of the Word—that will endure. "The grass withers, the flower fades, but the word of the Lord abides forever."

In the beautiful movie about the scholar and theologian C. S. Lewis called *Shadowlands*, Howard, the young son of Joy, who will become C. S. Lewis' wife, upon meeting Lewis for the first time thrusts out for an autograph a copy of one of Lewis' novels of fantasy, whose narrative carries treasures of theology.

Lewis takes the book and writes on its cover page these words, "The magic never ends." That is the way it is with preaching. Frail human beings speak to frail human beings. Words, sometimes carefully crafted and sometimes only loosely related, form transactions of grace across space as soul speaks to soul. But the magic that makes it all happen is what we call the Holy Spirit, who takes our words spoken, and our words heard, and magic happens. God is present in power to restore our souls, to renew our flagging spirits, to correct our ways, to urge us to do justly, to exercise full citizenship in the City of God. And that does not just happen one Sunday with one sermon. It goes on and on. "The magic never ends." That is the promise. That is the reality. That is how the church comes to be the Church of Jesus Christ. No wonder we are grateful when such magic happens; it is what we live by.

Thanks to Elam Davies and John Buchanan for helping to make it happen in one church in one city. Thanks to all those on the staff of Fourth Church and beyond who preach. And thanks be to God for the gift and the privilege of preaching the gospel—again and again and again and again.

—*Jack L. Stotts*
President, Austin Presbyterian Theological Seminary
Austin, Texas

Sermons
for the
City

Part One

Elam Davies

Pastor, 1961–1984

ELAM DAVIES WAS BORN IN WALES AND EDUCATED AT THE University of Wales and Cambridge University, England. He served two pastorates in Wales before being called to the First Presbyterian Church of Bethlehem, Pennsylvania, in 1951. He became pastor of the Fourth Presbyterian Church of Chicago in September 1961. Noted throughout the world for his eloquent preaching, Dr. Davies has been named one of "seven star preachers" in the United States by *Time* magazine and one of Chicago's "ten most powerful preachers" by the *Chicago Tribune*. He retired in May 1984 and was named pastor emeritus of Fourth Church. Dr. Davies and his wife Grace presently reside in Bethlehem, Pennsylvania.

ONE

On Finding God Where You Least Expect Him

I resolved that while I was with you I would think of nothing but Jesus Christ—Christ nailed to the cross.
1 Corinthians 2:2 (NEB)

WE LIVE IN A DAY WHEN YOU CAN have religion to your taste and theology to your liking. If the idea of God offered you in one context doesn't suit, and your appetite is jaded and you want a change, don't worry! There are thirty-nine varieties at least!

Of course, this is nothing new. In every generation people have been offered plausible substitutes for the Christian faith and remarkably well-camouflaged distortions of the biblical confession, but what surprises you again and again is the kind of person who is taken in by it, and the unquestioning, unthinking, emotionally controlled attitude of mind which falls for that which "works" in spite of the repeated demonstration of the pragmatic approach.

Paul came to Corinth determined that while he was there, he would think of nothing but Jesus Christ—Christ nailed to the cross. To most of us this would appear narrow or dull because, if the truth were known, we like other kinds of religion better.

Take, for example, *the Jesus captured by romanticized history*. You know what I mean, the Jesus of the picture books which are supposed to represent what the gospel proclaims "the pale Galilean," as Renan called him; or "the far-off mystic of the Galilean Hills," as Lord Morley described him; the haloed harmless helper of people, as many painters have depicted him; this mock-modest, meek and mild messenger, as sentimental hymns have liltingly proclaimed him; this sorrowful, perhaps sullen, specimen of humanity which our hate-the-world puritanical consciences have seen in him. To many, this is the Jesus of history, but I want to tell you this morning that described thus he is the Jesus of poor history, unscholarly history—really not history at all.

Or take, again, *the Jesus captured by contemporary religion*, the unreal image of the stained-glass window; the propagator and preserver of the neat little franchise that goes under the name of a successful church; the ubiquitous guest of all the groups that meet to talk and talk and talk religion; the smiling approver of the Sunday morning crowd, or of the religious conference that meets to pass resolutions and no more, or of the council which gets so bureaucratically top-heavy that it is likely to topple over by the weight of this deadness.

In the heart of the Bavarian mountains we visited a small glass factory, fronted by a fine shop which sold all kinds of wares created by expert craftsmen. There were the finished vessels for use and decoration, and there were the venerable religious images. It was all so neat, so beautiful, so attractive. "Would you like to see where these are produced?" asked our guide; and a few seconds and short passages later, we turned up in an unprepossessing workshop where older men and younger apprentices were at work, shaping the glass on wheels on which drops of water fell along an untidy piece of string, and cutting into the product with care and precision and superb skill.

What struck us about the workshop was its contrast to the display of fine glass on the street. We had come from delicacy to dirt, from show to struggle, from near perfection to painstaking effort, from tidiness to tawdriness. Here the cutting edge replaced the costly exhibition, and years of learning came into focus rather than the dazzling moment of achievement. The venerable images belonged there; they were only displayed elsewhere.

The Jesus captured by modern religion is often the Jesus of display. He is there to be admired. We want to forget that he belongs where the cutting edge of life is, where the slow and tedious process of life's apprenticeship is followed, where the sparks fly, and the constant boring drip of life's tediousness seems to follow a shaggy but undeviating line. Thus it is that religion becomes dull, and the pursuit of it a pastime for these who are so inclined.

Or take, again, *the Christ made captive by our piousness,* the Christ who never escapes the coils of our subjectivism, who is never bigger than our experience of him, who is never greater than our capacity to understand him. What a small Christ he is—how utterly unattractive!

In his book *The Offensive Traveler* [Knopf, 1964], V. S. Pritchett has many interesting side comments about the countries he visited and the people he saw. In Bulgaria, for instance, he met a man "who had a set of steel teeth which gave him an official and ferocious look. He had the flat face of a Byzantine saint. He didn't understand a word we were saying; he uttered his chorus: 'All men are brothers all over the world!' Every time our nouns and infinitives failed, and we were reduced to pathos of dumb animals, he started up ecstatically, 'all men are brothers. . . .'"

Something like this happens, too, when we meet the too saintly who seek to capture Christ by their specialized pious jargon. They are unable to communicate with us, and we with them. Our nouns and adjectives and the use of our infinitives are so different when we discuss religion with them, and we are left with fine sounding clichés which do nothing but increase our frustration. By such techniques Christ is relegated to the "in-group" and this will never do. "I resolved while I was with you," the apostle says, "I would think of nothing but Jesus Christ—Christ nailed to the cross!" Did you hear that? Christ nailed to the cross, not then but now, not in history only, but in all of life as it is struggled with, and fought in, day by day.

When Paul spoke of "Christ nailed to the cross," he was proclaiming and interpreting the most central thing we can say about Jesus. Mark, not the only thing, but the most central, namely, that wherever life in its contradictoriness is, he is, and wherever sin in its ugliness is, he is. Wherever man at his worst is, he is, and where he is, God is! He was raised to a throne with a crown of thorns on his head, on a city filth dump, outside the walls of decency, on a cross around which love and lust were gathered, where gracious people watched and gamblers threw dice! And all the while, God was there, divinely active, stupendously reaching out to reconcile to himself the hateful, the lustful, and the vengeful!

Men and women, can you hear what I am saying? I am saying what the New Testament is saying, that the place you find God is in the whole of life, among the spiritual and among the sensual, in the midst of the beauty and the bawdiness of existence. Where else? Try to keep him within the dingy pages of history, try to hold him within the hallowed walls of tradition, try to confine him within the circumscribing limits of religious individualism, and you will end up not finding him at all. "He was crucified, dead and buried," and that's what's happening to Christ now. He is in the world where the victimized are struggling for recognition, where the frustrated and perverted sex-obsessed are looking for meaning. He is in the world of dirty politics and vicious polemics, in the world of gang warfare and juvenile delinquency, of dope addition and drunkenness, of broken homes and battered lives, and he is in the world nailed to a cross, and where he is nailed to a cross God is—loving and reconciling! Reconciling! Never forget that!

With what quickened step and bated breath we walked along the art-laden corridors of the Vatican, eager to look at the beauties of the Sistine Chapel for the first time. It seemed that we knew what to expect, and yet, we didn't. There was both excitement and exasperation as we stepped in through its north door, finding ourselves in the midst of a milling crowd, most of whom were gaping vacantly at the pictures of this rectangular hall, probably the most overdecorated room in the world! The drone of the countless guides, the din of the babbling crowd, the bored detachment of the must-see-it tourist, served to combine with the ill-lighted masterpieces of Renaissance genius to create an initial effect which at once was overwhelming and discouraging.

But in a while the beauty of the place took over, and as each fresco was looked at more carefully, the wonder of it all gripped you. Who could but be moved by the magnificence of the vaulted ceiling entirely covered with the masterpieces of Michelangelo? How imagination could run wild and reconstruct the figures of the artist on his back performing the exhausting commission of the irascible Julius II, upon whose head, it is said, he dripped "accidentally" more than one blob of paint! But it was on Michelangelo's work at sixty that our attention was riveted, the great altar piece of the last judgment. "All the medieval horrors of Dante's *Inferno*, all the fire and brimstone of Savonarola's sermons are in the violent apocalyptic vision of punishment, in which even the blessed seemed damned."

We sat there for a long time looking, both fascinated and horrified, at the pained expressions, the twisted bodies, the writing souls of this colossal composition, which time and candle and smoke and incense have darkened, but have never obliterated this stupendous testimony to the agony of tormented genius. Then, suddenly we saw it. Against the backdrop of the darkest abyss and wildest terror, against the vision of the most hopeless condition, the bottom of the hell of hells, was flung the shadow of a cross. Whether by design or by accident, who knows, but the shadow of the massive crucifix on the chapel's altar was cast on the nether regions of that huge painting as if to defy Michelangelo's final agony, as if to deny the abysmal sense of damnation for man, as if to say "God is here, too, in the very hell of human existence," and where he is, he reconciles in amazing, redeeming love.

Can you understand what I am trying to say? No, I am not developing any theory of a larger hope, or propounding the doctrine of universalism. I am saying that sitting in the Sistine Chapel, the shadow of the cross thrown over Michelangelo's abyss made my heart sing, and I knew that there was no abysmal corner of life where God is not, no hopeless condition at the heart of which he is not found, no final crisis of which he is not a part in reconciling love.

In a book called *The Caring Church*, its editor Peter Smith, by a series of anecdotes, recalls the maxim of Bonhoeffer, "That the church is her true self only when she exists for humanity," or the late William Temple, who claimed that the church ought to be the institution which exists "primarily for the benefit of nonmembers." Probably the finest tribute in this book was paid to Father Joe of Stepney, London, by a reformed prostitute. Putting it the only way she knew, she said, "I owe that good priest a hell of a lot"; and the popular Scottish religious writer, William Barclay, adds, "Blessed is the man who can receive a testimonial like that!"

Blessed is the church, too! The church that cares, that confronts its members with the crucified, risen Christ, and sends them out into the world, only to find that he is there first, involved to the limits in its blackest situations, showing the limitless grace of God, beckoning us to work with him in interpreting it! This is what "Christ nailed to the cross" means. You will find God where you least expect him.

—September 27, 1964

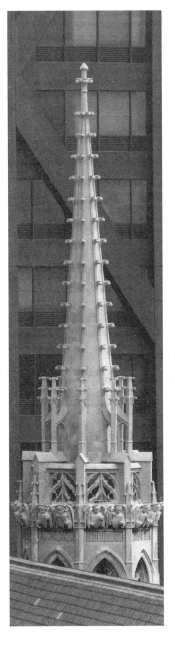

Two

The Protest of a Modern Palm Sunday

And as he rode along, they spread their garments on the road. As he was now drawing near, at the descent of the Mount of Olives, the whole multitude of the disciples began to rejoice and praise God with a loud voice for all the mighty works that they had seen. . . . And some of the Pharisees in the multitude said to him, "Teacher, rebuke your disciples." He answered, "I tell you, if these were silent, the very stones would cry out."

Luke 19:36–37, 39–40 (RSV)

IN THE YEAR 1968, A PROCESSION close to Palm Sunday was being planned in the city of Memphis, Tennessee, and ironically the central figure in it was another who was called "King"—Martin Luther King Jr. Of course, the parade was illegal—but so was the first Palm Sunday effort. It was against the law of the occupying Roman government. To participate in an open demonstration, to greet a rebel as if he were a monarch, was nothing more than an open invitation to lawlessness and insurrection. Such pestilent upstarts must be silenced.

And worse, it was shamefully illegal in the eyes of the orthodox good people, those like you and me who set so much store in order and decency, respect for

11

tradition and decorum. "Rebuke them" came the urgent request to Jesus. Shut those shouting ones up! How vulgar, how noisy, how blasphemous they are! Can a messiah riding on a donkey, making a fool of himself in the eyes of decent people, be any better than a modern would-be savior, who puts himself at the head of a procession of garbage collectors who persist in shouting "Amen" and "Hallelujah" and spread what we disdainfully describe as their cotton pickin' garments before *their* King?

No! Before you are affronted by what I'm saying, I'm not contending that what happened in Memphis is the same thing that happened on the way to Jerusalem. Jesus wasn't staging a "demonstration" in our modern sense of the word. We're not taking a leaf out of the book of the liberals of the 1930s who delighted in equating Jesus with Gandhi, and no doubt would take equal delight in making a great civil rights leader the savior of men.

What I am saying is that there is sufficient in common between the parade of the first and the present Palm Sunday to make us stop and ask, "Whose side are we on? The palm wavers or the cold-water throwers, the garment spreaders or the grumblers?"

I have no doubt that because of our incurable religious sentimentality, we shall stoutly declare that we are on the side of the former. After all, didn't we sing a few moments ago,

> Hosanna loud hosanna,
> The little children sang;
> Through pillared court and temple
> The lovely anthem rang. . . .

But it wasn't all so lovely and so pretty. This was no sentimentalist riding on the foal of an ass. He was as hard as nails. From the very start of his mission, he had angered people. He had stirred many of them to deep hatred. "'The Spirit of the Lord is upon me, because he has anointed me to preach good news to the poor. He has sent me to proclaim release to the captives and recovering of sight to the blind, to set at liberty those who are oppressed . . .'" (Luke 4:18, RSV).

That wasn't sweet religious talk, you know. It had political undertones, economic undertones, social undertones, and the people of the day knew it. They took him to the city hill and tried to hurl him over its precipice, and their sympathizers were in the crowd this Palm Sunday. They were only biding their time, only waiting their chance. There was only one way to deal with this rabble-rouser, this dangerous left-winger, this peace-talking agitator!

Mind you, they wouldn't have touched him with a finger. They were not of that kind. Only the pathological, the perverted, would do the act—the sick ones. But, while they wouldn't hammer any nails or look down a scope and pull a modern trigger, they were all for shutting him up. Suddenly, these resentful ones mixed with the disciples and the children, and the garbage collectors and the ghetto dwellers, who had nothing to lose but their captivity and nothing to shed but their rags. They joined with the least and the last and the lost, not as marchers but as lookers-on, and they felt nothing but contempt for the hallelujah screams and the hosanna cries, and the praise-the-Lord ejaculations.

And when the King came, he knew the chance he was taking. He knew that some of his fellow nationals thought he was a maudlin moderate, or worse, a worthless weakling. Didn't the powers-that-be understand one word only—violence? Hadn't the Romans built their empire on the sweat of slaves? Fire must be fought with fire, they said, and sword with sword.

Even one of his disciples was planning to liquidate him because, of all crazy things, he kept on saying that you must resist passively, you must be willing to suffer and to die without fighting back.

There was something awesome about his determination to go to his "Memphis." After all, he was only thirty-three. He wanted to live, too. But like one of his followers last week, he had climbed the mountain and seen the promised land and was ready to face what-ever came. You couldn't have predicted the nails exactly, any more than you could have predicted the sniper's bullet that swept the martyr off his feet on a Tennessee motel balcony. But the most dis-astrous factor was not what happened, unbelievable as it is; it was the mood and the climate in which it could take place.

I wonder on whose side we would have been—the hosanna side or the hate side, the blessed-is-he side or the blast-him side? Of course, we don't all hate in the same way. Some of us are very refined about it. We're not like the white taxi driver who last Friday, seeing a rude and resentful band of black young people pushing over pedestrians in the Loop, remarked to his passenger: "We should have done it fifteen years ago: lined every nigger against the wall and shot him! We'd have saved all this!" We don't hate like that, do we? Or *do we*?

And, of course, we pride ourselves that we're not like the psychotic and violent Stokely Carmichael, who Judas-fashion sells his nation into deeper despair by urging the members of his race to "go get a gun," to take to the barricades. But we're not much for change either, are we? We lump the Luther Kings with the Rap Browns and failing to understand the nonviolent crusade of the former, we've resented it as much as the wild extravagances of the latter; and it may be that we have lost our chance now.

The A.D. 68 King didn't live to see his parade through, but the A.D. 33 King did. He saw the ancient capital city of his nation in the distance, its magnificent temple gleaming in the dazzling sun, and he wept. "O Jerusalem, Jerusalem [Washington, Washington?], would that even today you knew the things that made for peace. But now they are hid from your eyes. For the days shall come upon you, when your enemies will cast up a bank about you and surround you, and hem you in on every side, and dash you to the ground, you and your children within you, and they will not leave one stone upon another, because you did not know the time of your visitation. . . ."

What incredible words from the so-called meek and mild man who rode the donkey down the Palm Sunday road. But it happened, just as he said it would, and it could happen again. Did you not hear an echo of his words in Memphis last week, in Chicago, New York, Washington?

Men and women, why are we so blind to the lessons of history? Why are we so stupid as to think that we can get away with oppression or injustice, or plain indifference? We can't stop the march of events. We're not going to silence the cry of God's excluded ones. "Master, rebuke your followers," said the "stand-patters" and the "status-quoers," who wanted nothing but peace to enjoy selfishly what they had. "Rebuke them?" Jesus asked incredulously. "I tell you, if these were silent, the very stones would cry out."

They've started to cry out already, haven't they? The stones, I mean! They cry out as they are hurled from clenched fists. The "land of the free and the home of the brave" is an armed camp. Trucks full of federal troops ride down our beautiful Lake Shore Drive. I never thought I would see the day when police and soldiers with guns at the ready would be walking up and down outside of my home! Behind Fourth Church the sky is red with the frustrated fires of reverse racism.

You don't have to wait for America to be attacked by the enemies without. It will fall, unless we wake up, by the hand of enemies within. And these enemies within are not one-colored only. They are white and black, whose hate feeds on hate, whose resentment breeds resentment. For some it will take the refined way of doing nothing and caring less. For others, it will take the road of loot and shoot. There's no difference between them!

On this day of national mourning and commemoration for the life of the first world-known Negro martyr, we may well be found being ashamed in the least radical way. There is no doubt at all that we shall gravely decry the young white suspect who looked through the telescopic lens of the Remington pump-rifle, saw his victim and silenced him forever. But we'll excuse ourselves and say, "It was just one." So it was, but there is more to it than that.

And we shall, so predictably, piously shake our heads over the outbreak of violence these past few days, but we'll comfort ourselves and say, "It is the work of the few." So it is, but there is more to it than that.

Well might we be ashamed.

If we're not collectively guilty, we are collectively responsible. The name of our fair country has been besmirched once again. Our hearts should sag with the Stars and Stripes at half-mast. But the publicity will pass, and Martin Luther King Jr., having secured for himself a supremely deserved place in history's hall of fame, will be spoken of only as a memory. And what will happen as the result of the parade, say, this protest parade of a modern Palm Sunday? What will happen to you and to me, to our attitudes and concerns and conduct in the days to come? What will happen here in Fourth

Church in relation to our neighbors, deprived and dispossessed?
   Listen to another Palm Sunday hymn which has succeeded in cutting the sentiment.

> Draw nigh to Thy Jerusalem, O Lord
> Thy faithful people cry with one accord:
> Ride on in triumph; Lord behold we lay
> Our passions, lusts, and *proud wills* in thy way!
> Hosanna! welcome to our hearts! for here
> Thou hast a temple, too, as Zion dear,
> O enter in, dear Lord, unbar the door,
> And in that temple dwell forevermore.

   But if we ask him to enter in, let's not expect him to come accommodatingly. That's not how he entered the temple on the first Palm Sunday, any more than Dr. King entered the sacred precincts of the Memphis establishment last week. Let us never forget that there is a strong element of militancy about nonviolence, especially when it assails our prejudices and our cherished privileges. God grant that we may know the day of our visitation!

—April 7, 1968

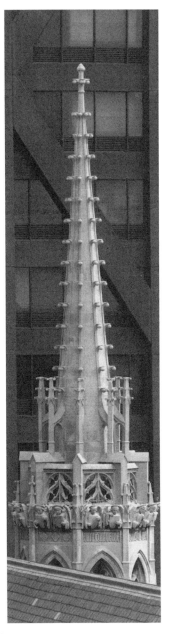

THREE

What Jesus Has to Say about Our Anxieties

"Therefore do not be anxious about tomorrow, for tomorrow will be anxious for itself. Let the day's own trouble be sufficient for the day."

Matthew 6:34 (RSV)

WHAT DOES JESUS HAVE TO SAY about our anxieties? Perhaps we could understand his teaching, if we first responded to another question. What do *we* have to say about them? Most of us try to play the amateur psychologist from time to time, and so it is important to clarify our thoughts and define our views.

Broadly speaking, *anxieties*, from our modern point of view, can be categorized in three ways: pathological, neurotic, and ordinary. When we speak about "pathological anxieties," we are in a sphere where everyone who is not an expert is out of his or her depth. These are anxieties which are created by chemical insufficiencies, neurological malfunctions, or psychological abnormalities. Generally, these are the concerns of specialists in the field,

17

though if we suspect that someone we know is victim to this pathological form of anxiety, we should be extraordinarily careful in our choice of the expert to deal with it.

When Jesus spoke about handling our anxiety, he wasn't primarily thinking about this form of it, though it was not altogether absent from his frame of reference. Where the New Testament speaks about "casting out devils," we speak of healing psychoses.

Then, again, there are our "neurotic anxieties." These arise from imbalance or maladjustment in our emotional life, and in different ways we have all experienced them. In our ordinary language, we describe ourselves as being "worrywarts" or being victims to squirrel-cage thinking, or having "butterflies in our stomach" which never cease from flitting, or waking with almost explosive regularity at 3 A.M., or just being "uptight" all the time.

As we said, few of us have escaped one form or another of this "anxiety neurosis," as we frequently describe it, and it can range from the dangerous, to the serious, to the commonplace. Jesus, while not attempting to psychoanalyze us, does have something to say about this kind of anxiety.

It is the third form as seen by us that I call "ordinary" anxiety. W. H. Auden, who recently died in Vienna, described our age as an "Age of Anxiety." Contemporary novel writers seem to be wallowing in concern over "cosmic anxiety," the vague feeling of misgiving we all have (which can lead to total despair) when we sense our precarious foothold in the universe or in life itself. It is accentuated when a nation is subjected to a series of traumatic shocks, or the world appears to be teetering on the brink of disaster because of another international bust-up. Add to that sense of anxiety the many forms which plague our daily lives about health, or jobs, our future, about our children, our loves and hates, our personal relationships, about adolescence, middle age and old age, about retrenchment or retirement, about inflation and personal security. Anxiety knows no generation gap. It leaps back and forth like a fire across any barrier, setting alight a temporary flame of concern or a brushfire of panic, or a combustible explosion of despair.

I need not go on. Jesus has plenty to say about all this, and it is precisely on these facts that we shall concentrate, and then work backwards to that second form of anxiety which borders on the neurotic.

Well then, what has Jesus to say about our ordinary anxieties?

Let me remind you again how often I have advised you never to underestimate the incredible shrewdness of Jesus, especially as a judge of the human predicament. I said that he will not psychoanalyze you, but he will confront you with some straightforward psychological considerations.

Reflect on what some of these are. First, he bids us live in day-tight compartments. No one can doubt the commonsense wisdom of the maxim, "Let the day's own trouble be sufficient for itself." Ideally, that's what any wise counselor will tell you. "Don't buy trouble!" We often say, "Don't worry, it may never happen!" But Jesus didn't say that. Rather, his counsel was "Don't worry even *if it is going to happen,*" because your anxiety can't change a thing. You're short and you want to be tall, you're fat and you want to be thin, you're sick and you want to get well, you don't have much and you want more, you're underachieving and you want to do better? "Try it the 'worry way,'" Jesus says. Sit down and worry yourself into physical shape, economic security, success, and see what will happen! The desired result will usually be in inverse ratio to the amount of anxiety you expend on it. Of course, Jesus wasn't saying don't plan, or prepare, or take precaution, or strive. He was simply affirming what we all know but almost never acknowledge in practice, that anxiety debilitates us, saps our energies, undermines our resolves, decimates our achievements, and cheats us of our rewards.

With a twinkle in his eye, he says (if ever you doubted the humor of Jesus), "Do not be anxious about tomorrow, for tomorrow will be anxious about itself." Notice, will you, that he does not say "Tomorrow *you* will be anxious about yourself," but *tomorrow* will be.

Time heals, we say, and this is often true, but it *can't* handle its own problems. That's why we say that "history repeats itself." And if the days can't handle themselves, how do you think they can handle your troubles, or solve your problems?

You must learn to live in day-tight compartments, the Master says, because (in effect) God has planned the night to follow the day. You must train yourself to say, "This too shall pass."

"It sounds so trite," you say. Yes it does. "And so utterly sim-plistic," someone adds. Did you say simplistic? Careful now! Don't be fool enough to accuse Jesus of that. He gives simple direction, yes! Simplistic, never!

He wasn't advocating the power of positive thinking, though Dr. Peale is right in pointing out that this can help immeasurably. And believe me, Jesus wasn't offering a short course in positive mental attitude techniques as a sure key to success.

Indeed, Jesus would be swift to point out that harping on suc-cess as the only thing that counts in life can be the most diabolical cause of anxiety of all. It's the devil's breeding ground for it. You *must be* an achiever, a winner, a hundred-percenter, no matter in what sphere, religion, morality, your business, your profession. How ghastly!

Don't you realize, men and women, that the drive, the over-whelming urge, the implacable demand of the monsters "Success" and "Possession" can literally kill us?

God created the night to end the frantic activity or the frenetic search of the day, and when it closes in on you, you need a guardian for your body, your mind, your spirit!

Do you remember your childhood prayers?

> Lord, keep me safe this night
> Secure from all my fears
> May angels guard me while I sleep
> 'Till morning light appears.

> Now I lay me down to sleep;
> I pray the Lord my soul to keep.
> If I should die before I wake,
> I pray the Lord my soul to take.

Remember the commercial: "Today is the first day of the rest of your life . . . start it well. . . ." "I wish I could," someone says wistfully. "But yesterday drags over, and tomorrow looms large. . . ."

That's when Jesus begins to dig deeper and work back (or down, if you wish), into anxiety as neurosis. We are not speaking of the commonplace recurrence of anxieties now, but of ANXIETY in caps, and unless it is pathological in the most technical sense, Jesus has something to say about that. He adds two further considerations to the one we have been talking about, namely that we should live in day-tight compartments. Either we want too much, or we trust too little.

The Master speaks about food and drink and clothing, not in an otherworldly way—he was no ascetic ("The Son of Man came eating and drinking"), and not in a disparaging way, as some do about material things—he was no dullard. His point about the lilies not "toiling or spinning" was not a jab at the work ethic, but a demand that you admit that their magnificence doesn't arise from frantic and pointless struggle.

He makes another of those "simple" comments which are explosive with reality. "Surely life is more than food, the body more than clothes." In other words, "Surely, you count more than the next suit, car, carpet, or gold coins!" What's the good of it all, if they possess you and you're not around to appreciate them. What will we sacrifice for the heaped-up pile? Prestige? Position? Health, honor, the sheer joy of just being?

And then with unerring analysis, he pierces deeply into those recesses of our souls where "get" and "get-away-with-it," greed and grab, really begin. He asks us why we have such a poor concept of God. That's right! He insists on knowing why we are worse than heathen. He tells us, if we listen, why we are almost possessed by the demonic in our mad scramble to get and get more—whatever it may be. *We don't trust our Father in heaven.*

With almost divine absurdity Jesus asks, "Are ye not worth more than many sparrows?" How do *you* answer that question?

—*October 14, 1973*

FOUR

One Nation under God

THERE IS VERY LITTLE ATHEISM IN America if our public opinion polls are to be trusted. Most people within the United States believe in some kind of god or another. Atheism, as you know, is the denial of the existence or the relevance of God. And theism, dropping the *a*, is an affirmation that you cannot understand life without belief in a god. So there are more theists in America by far than there are atheists. As a matter of fact, if you're going to believe Gallup and Yankelovich and CBS and the *New York Times* and all their polling of public opinion, you're going to come to the conclusion that the apostle Paul might have said of modern-day America much as he said of ancient Athens, "Men and women, I perceive that in all

22

things you are scrupulously religious."

The Pledge of Allegiance, the Declaration of Independence, the Congressional prayers given at the opening of the session, the words on our coins, give formal authentication to our belief "In God We Trust." And if this is the case, let me begin by calling attention to the fact that when we talk about "one nation under God," we are talking about *one nation*. Not one race, not one tribe, although the word nation, you must know, can be highly ambiguous. Take this definition, for example, from the dictionary: "Nation: a distinct race or people characterized by common descent, language, or history. Usually organized as a separate political state and occupying a definite geographical territory." Now you and I could easily overlook the either/or in that definition. You see, the United States is not a distinct race, is it? But it is a distinct people. It is not characterized by a common descent, is it? But it has a common history.

Our nationhood does not depend on color, does it? But it stems from certain marked beliefs and the cohesions that take place around those beliefs. What are these marked beliefs around which our cohesion takes place? Well, we repeat them from time to time: that those who belong to the nation, whatever order they are in society, whatever tongue they speak as they cross the limits of the shore, have certain inalienable rights. And mark you, that these rights don't inhere simply in the personhood of the one concerned, but they have been endowed that way by their Creator. It is God that has given us the inalienable right to human dignity. *You* don't confer it on anyone! Laws only express it! It is God who gives it.

And let us beware lest we strip, by any policy or any program, that dignity which belongs to personhood, because God has no favorites. You know that. You think he has? You think that he has set certain people in certain classes and other people in less desirable classes? That he has blessed people with abundance of wealth and deprived others of the necessities of existence? Don't fool yourself, and may I not fool myself. God has no favorites. He causes his sun to shine on the just and the unjust, on the rich and the poor as we divide them, on the acceptable and the unacceptable, on the included and the excluded. There are no exclusions, in God's concept, of people. "One nation, with liberty and justice for all."

I have spoken before of the first time I came to the shores of
America (on my own on that occasion) in 1948 when the tired and
the hungry of Europe were coming with me; and we sailed for the
first time ever, most of us, on that old Cunard ship, past the Statue
of Liberty; and people fell to their knees crying, as the proud lady
held up her torch and welcomed them to her shores. And years
later we went over on a small boat to the island and we climbed all
over the Statue of Liberty and so did many others—up the stairs,
along the arm. Seeing it from the boat gave it an aura which was
magnificent. Climbing over it in our pettifogging little way, we
reduced it to something which was manageable. And you and I are
likely to repeat that again and again. Sometimes we see at a distance "with freedom, liberty and justice for all," and then, in our
daily lives, we climb all over these beliefs, and by our crude and
crass ways deny them even for people in the same bus, in the same
shop, in the same office, in the same school, in the same church.

And let's never forget that we're an indivisible nation. And
that indivisibility has to be seen in a variety of contexts, most particularly in the day in which we live, when there are people of alien
tongues and different features clamoring to our shores again,
looking for the light of that Statue of Liberty. I heard the contempt
of someone the other day who said "if they don't do anything to
stop those Cubans coming into this country. . . ." What? To stop
them? I wonder what would have happened if the benighted and
the tired and the hungry and the forgotten in times past had been
left at Ellis Island. *Indivisible.*

There's a British astronomer/physicist who is a professor at
the Institute for Advanced Studies in Princeton, one of the world's
great thinkers, an Englishman by the name of Freeman Dyson; and
Freeman Dyson has written a book recently called *Disturbing the
Universe* [Harper & Row, 1979]. He became a citizen of the United
States in about 1960. And Dyson talks about going to Trenton, New
Jersey, for his citizenship papers. He says that making his commit-
ment to the country in this setting somehow didn't mean very
much to him because it was so formal, so stereotyped. But, "On the
Fourth of July [in 1962] I went with my wife and our two youngest
children to watch the fireworks on the ellipse behind the White
House. A big crowd was there, predominantly black, sitting on the

grass and waiting for the show. We sat down among them."

Now the man who's writing this is one of the most brilliant thinkers, physicists, astronomers; not a man who's likely to be taken in simply by side shows. "Our children were soon running around with the others. Then came the fireworks. After the official fireworks were over, the crowd was allowed to let off unofficial fireworks. Everybody seemed to have brought something. And the black children all had little rockets or Catherine wheels or sparklers and were shouting with joy as they blazed away," says Dyson. "Only our children sat quiet and sad, because we had not brought them anything. But suddenly one of the black children came up to us and gave our children a fistful of sparklers so that they could join in the fun. That moment"—now this a very sober man who's talking—"that moment, rather than the ceremony in Trenton, was the beginning of my true citizenship. It was then that I knew for sure we were at home in America." Indivisible, men and women, indivisible whichever way you cross the barriers. Indivisible. And woe betide us whether we try to divide our country according to color or creed or background or social status or wealth.

All right. If we are one nation, let me look at the second fact, let me direct your attention to the fact that we are one nation *under God*. Under God. Earlier we observed that statistically, atheism is absent in America. We forget the psalmist's comment that the atheist is not the one who mouths the derogatory comments about faith. The atheist is the one who says it in his heart. "The fool," said the psalmist, had said in his heart—in his heart, remember—"there is no God." He may not have said it with his lips, he may have never formulated it in his mind, but in his heart he said there is no God. And he wasn't a fool because of his credo, he was a fool because of his conscience—or rather his lack of it. He didn't have much, and he didn't care. There was an element of unscrupulousness in his attitude toward his fellow men.

He might have fumed and fought, if he were living in our day, for prayers in schools for children, and denied the cry of the hungry and the poor and the wretched. That's what a fool does. Mark you, it is important that people stand for a reintroduction at all levels of our life, beginning with the schools, of the affirmations which basically and fundamentally are at the heart of our heritage. So, with you, I am for prayer in schools. But let's watch out that we're not for prayer in schools, just the mouthing of the petitions or the worship, while at the same time in our heart we have segregated ourselves from human need and degradation and we've set ourselves off in a neat little island of our own fantasy delighting in all the blessings which God has bestowed upon us, while others struggle and are broken by life. It's in his heart that the fool said there was no God.

And "one nation under God" means under his goodness and his severity. Under his blessing and his judgment. Under his power as well as his providence. And if we are aware that we are under God's judgment as well as his blessing, if we are aware that we are "one nation under God," then I'll tell you something . . . there is no room for vulgar boasting or crass, odious comparisons. They are revealed for what they are. Let us stop, for God's sake, in the name of that which is part of our heritage, saying that we have more automobiles and more televisions and more dishwashers than anyone else in the world. Who cares? Especially if you're out there scratching for enough food to live for the next six hours. What unseemly boasting it is—that infantile wish, not just to be number one, but to be the only one! God's judgment is swift on that, men and women, let me tell you, swift. "Under God" means that we recognize that we can either be under God or under the demonic, the demonic powers of darkness, the satanic powers.

So the Empire strikes back, doesn't it? It always strikes back. You don't have to go to theology and the Bible for a division of darkness and light, of God and the demonic, you're entertained by it. And you and I should know that when Darth Vader, the arch-villain of *Star Wars,* sneaked out through the back hatch, when the good guys had just destroyed the Empire's death star and were busy decorating their heroes, we should have known that if Darth Vader sneaked out, massive trouble was in store.

The Empire strikes back—it always does. And in the sequel, Luke Skywalker is told that he must feel the Force around him. The Force. The Force! But Luke's not good at that and even though he sees the Force in action, our hero says, "I don't believe it! I don't believe it!" And his instructor answers quite bluntly, "That is why you fail."

That is why we fail! We don't believe it. We don't believe in the dark forces of the Empire and we don't believe in the magnificent power of God. We don't believe it unless we face the fact that there is no neutrality in the battle of life, and there is no neutrality in the battle for nationhood in the United States. We can't sit on the sidelines. God has loosed the fateful lightning of his terrible swift sword and his truth is marching on. You might think of the sword as Luke Skywalker's light sword, I don't care. And you may think of the satanic forces as the Empire, I don't care. And of God as the Force, I don't care. The struggle is still the same whatever idiom you use—and you and I cannot be on the sidelines.

So let us not hug our blessings to ourselves. Let's not congratulate ourselves that we are living in such a great, fine, noble country—all of which it is—if there is an atheism in our hearts which propels us in a lack of compassion and a censoriousness and a certain downgrading of anyone who is not one of us. "Under God" does not mean protection of the status quo; "under God" means going forth in risky fashion to recreate our image.

"With liberty and justice for all." "Indivisible." "Under God."

> Mine eyes have seen the glory of the coming of the Lord;
> He is trampling out the vintage where the grapes of wrath are
>   stored;
> He hath loosed the fateful lightning of his terrible swift sword;
> His truth is marching on.

And just as Julia Ward Howe heard the tramp of the soldiers in Washington and wrote this "Battle Hymn of the Republic," so we can hear the sound of the distant armies of almighty God's avenging forces for good, which at last will overcome the empire of darkness.

—*July 6, 1980*

FIVE

When Revival Is Threatened by Rhetoric

From the day that the ark was lodged at Kiriath-jearim, a long time passed, some twenty years, and all the house of Israel lamented after the Lord. Then Samuel said to all the house of Israel, "If you are returning to the Lord with all your heart, then put away the foreign gods . . . from among you, and direct your heart to the Lord, and serve him only. . . ." And the people of Israel said to Samuel, "Do not cease to cry to the Lord our God for us, that he may save us from the hand of the Philistines."

1 Samuel 7:2–3, 8 (RSV)

THERE APPEARS TO BE A RENEWED interest in religion in the United States. Whether we can describe it as a revival is questionable, but this is certain:

> People are afraid and bewildered. They are seeking for fuller answers than ever before and God never fails to work in our moments of deepest need.

Revival is possible—an outpouring of God's Spirit in a dark hour of crisis. But remember this: whenever God is at work in a special way, other forces, demonic and divisive, are at work also. The greatest threat to truth is not untruth but half-truth; the most powerful assault on righteousness is not by open evil but by counterfeit goodness.

28

How powerfully Jesus knew this. He was always under pressure from the demonic. There was a sinister, satanic temptation which urged him to buy, dazzle, or coerce people, and all this came to him in moral technicolor. He could win—bring in God's kingdom if he would mastermind some power play for victory and manipulate people to this end. He adamantly refused, was hung on a cross, and was contemptuously dismissed as a failure.

The story we have taken from the Old Testament is an ancient tale about what people believed concerning the presence of God in their midst. This presence was symbolized by the Ark of the Covenant which later was to contain the Ten Commandments. If the ark was with them, then God was. If it was captured, disaster ensued.

We don't have to buy all these ancient beliefs, but there is sufficient substance in them to make us think. Like them we must acknowledge God's powerful presence in the whole of life. He is the God of our history as well as our personal experience. His presence means covenant and law, love and holiness.

We are linked to this ancient tale as the Ark of the Covenant (the symbol of God's presence) is seen again in the land. "There was a movement throughout Israel to follow the Lord." How beautiful! Revival at last! A return to spiritual values and verities! "So Samuel," says the Book, "addressed these words to the whole nation: 'If your return to the Lord is whole-hearted, banish the foreign false gods and Ashtaroth from your shrines. . . .'" In a word—"Watch out that your revival isn't a fake!"

Have you noticed, men and women, how religion has subtly become an issue in the present political campaign? Increasingly, it is being injected into the rhetoric of the stump. Code words abound:

- Born-again Candidates
- Moral Majority
- Separation of Church and State

the range of verbal confrontation is enormous.

What a mixed bag of headline themes! E.R.A., SALT II, abortion, gun control, classroom prayers, sexual preference, evolution, school busing, the Panama Canal, pornography. And, believe it or not, a debate over whether God hears or does not hear the prayer of a Jew.

No one is going to underestimate the importance of some of these concerns. The sad feature is that the genuine issues have been plastered by slogans, poisoned by invective, and rendered incredibly tawdry by charge and countercharge. Our religious and political beliefs are being made to look ludicrous, and we are in danger of becoming the laughingstock of the thinking world.

For this reason, I shall comment on none of the above. Rather, I will try to state simply what I consider to be the biblical principles about which we should be thinking, at a time when "a movement in the land to follow the Lord" is likely to be side-tracked into the demonic swamps of mindless absurdity. If the powers of darkness can make God's righteousness a vulgar joke, we're lost.

Let us face the facts. The Old Testament prophets, of whom Samuel was the precursor, were past masters at weaving God's purposes into the fabric of human history. And you can't have history without politics, sociology, psychology, and ethics.

When Jesus said, "Render unto Caesar the things that are Caesar's and unto God the things that are God's," he wasn't putting God and Caesar on the same level, or on par. Caesar may have certain things to say about God—he always has, but let's not forget that God emphatically has many things to say both about and to Caesar—not the least of which is that Caesar had better beware of God's righteous judgments in history.

And there is not the slightest doubt about what these judgments—the divine holy wrath—would be aimed at. *Idolatry*! Listen to Samuel: "Banish false gods . . . turn to the Lord with heart and mind and worship him alone."

Notice, men and women, heart and mind! There is an idolatry of feeling and an idolatry of thought. There are idols of desire and idols of intellect. There are fake gods of religion and of politics, pagan ideas and rhetoric.

Let us name a few forms of idolatry prevalent in our society. If I could use graphics to draw three columns, I would! Each would say the same thing in different ways:

Column 1	Column 2	Column 3
The idolatry of privilege	The god of exclusiveness	"I'll keep mine."
The idolatry of power	The god of tyranny	"Blow them off the face of the map."
The idolatry of pride	The god of hubris	"We're number one!"
The idolatry of prejudice	The god of racism	"One color under God . . ."
The idolatry of possession	The god of heartlessness	"Let them eat cake." (Marie Antoinette when the poor didn't have bread to eat.)
The idolatry of piousness	The god of lovelessness	"I thank Thee that I am not as others are. . . ."
The idolatry of passion	The god of lust	"What is right is what you feel good after. . . ."
The idolatry of personhood	The god of narcissism	"I love me, me, ME!"

What about immorality, you ask? It is *all* immorality! In the Scriptures, immorality is worshiping an idol—religious or secular—and telling the living God and others to "get lost" if they happen to stand in the way of our kind of piety or practice.

Does it need to be said so tritely? Immorality is the failure to be moral, not the failure to be formally correct. It is forgetting the demand to love God with our whole heart and mind and to love our neighbor as ourselves. Moses knew it! Samuel knew it! The prophets knew it! John the Baptist knew it! Jesus Christ knew it! How dare we be so blindly ignorant?

The biblical message is unmistakable. God's thoughts are not our thoughts. His ways are not our ways. We had better face the fact that Jesus Christ sees murder in smoldering anger, adultery in hidden fantasy, resentment in cheap and contemptuous name-calling ("Thou fool!") and vicious retaliation, thievery in robbing the poor, hypocrisy in paraded piety, hatred in the will to obliterate come what may.

So, far from condoning immorality, the Master widened and deepened its significance, so that not one of us could deny it in our own hearts. He was convinced that God's judgments were swiftest and surest when we were certain that *we only* are righteous, blameless, honest, pure, true, and good. There is something the Divine cannot stand—our massive cover-up of our moral rottenness by self-confident virtuosity and smug religiosity, whether we're Democrats, Republicans, or Independents. Only the grace of God can save us.

Well, does all this mean that we are to have no opinion about what is right and wrong, true and false, legitimate or illegitimate? Of course not. Being Christian forces us to make choices, some of which are unbelievably painful.

Frankly (and this is strictly my personal opinion), I find it passing strange when the cry for the "separation of church and state" is distorted into the demand that religion should be excluded from politics. In my view, evangelical-fundamentalist believers have a justifiable complaint when they say that for years they were derided for their indifference and otherworldliness, and now they are condemned because they decide formally to get involved in the political process.

For years the mainline churches, both Protestant and Catholic, have through their councils been up to their eyes in the political pool. When they wanted to baptize their pronouncements and actions with holy water, they called them "prophetic," and now, when others do the same thing, they are condemned as being unscrupulously partisan.

What concerns me is not their participation in the present national debate, but their thunderous silence on momentous issues central to the Christian proclamation of social righteousness—the plight of the least, the lost, the lonely, and the poor.

But let me return from opinion to biblical truth.

Of course, the Scriptures are blunt about the machinations of *some* people in authority, or those who aspire to authority, how some of them rob the poor, deceive the ignorant, cheat the weak, rip off the unsuspecting, and crush the defenseless. A moral God won't tolerate that!

Of course, the Scriptures have much to say about the worth of the individual and the sanctity of life. But, don't you think that a righteous God finds it offensive that we should calmly contemplate obliterating many more millions than we now can, while arguing over the right to life?

Of course, the Scriptures have much to say about doing a day's work for a negotiated wage, but they have something to say about those who come in at the eleventh hour, and those who don't have a chance to come in at all. God cares for the excluded, and we'd better pay attention to his care.

Of course, the Scriptures have much to say about parents and children, old age and youth. They reject the idea that old age is an actuarial disease. Rather it is a time when people should be honored and respected, and permitted to live in dignity after the long hard struggle of life. God isn't indifferent to the whimper of the neglected child, and he won't be deaf to the sigh of the aged, the forgotten, and the lonely. We had better find out on whose side he really is.

Of course, the Scriptures have much to say about personal honesty, purity, integrity, and the full mutual dependence of the sexes. God doesn't smile at our delinquencies. He smites and disciplines and judges. None of us can snow him with our platitudes or rationalizations, and certainly not with our self-righteous shibboleths.

But nowhere does Scripture give anyone the authority to tell, or to suggest or hint to another how he or she should vote. It urges us to participate fully in civic affairs that "in well doing, we may put to silence the ignorance of foolish men." But woe betide the preachers who use their pulpits as platforms, and the believers who use their credo as manifesto.

God is not impressed by our ecclesiasticism or true-believerism. Ask the Christ who rebuked the cynicism of the religious and political leaders of his day . . . who wept over Jerusalem, and rode on to die on the cross of Calvary, rather than trade obedience to God's will for the approval of the world.

Men and women, there is a sound of revival in the air. God forbid that we should smother it with our rhetoric, *including the rhetoric of this sermon*! Rather, let us swell the music by giving heed to the words of the people in Samuel's day; "Do not cease to pray for us to the Lord our God to save us from the power of the Philistines." Amen! and Amen!

—October 12, 1980

Six

The God in Whom
We Can Be Confident

Through him [Jesus Christ] you have confidence in God. . . .

1 Peter 1:21 (RSV)

"THE GOD IN WHOM WE CAN BE Confident"—did you think that that was a rather irreverent title? To speak of confidence in God smacks of a little insolence, doesn't it? Well, if the title disturbs you, substitute the words "faith" and "trust" for confidence. The God in whom we can trust. The God in whom we can have faith. The God in whom we can have confidence. But for every person that demurs, there are ten others who will leap to the thought that we may lack confidence in God. There are many people who ask, "Why me?" when life tumbles in on them. There are many people who ask, "What have I done?" when they are felled by accident or by disease. And there are some who ask, "What can I expect?" when they

35

are riddled and haunted by their own sense of guilt.

Does God indeed "get us for this"? Does he pay us back for our wrongdoing? Is he a celestial cop? (Yes, that's the word I used: "cop." In my native country I would have said "bobby.") Is he a celestial cop, or worse, a cosmic ogre? Is he? How preposterous.

Let me tell you what I am slowly learning at the closing years of my life, slowly learning about the opening words of the Lord's Prayer. "Hallowed be Thy name." We don't reverence God's name by using pious clichés. We don't reverence God's name by having fine feelings; and we don't hallow God's name by having exalted religious moods. And we don't reverence God's name simply by having religious observances, coming to church, or saying our prayers.

We begin to hallow God's name by refusing to demean him. Refusing to demean him, to make him less than we are, less than we are sometimes at our best and less than we are even sometimes at our worst. When I think of the things with which we credit God, we wouldn't credit a scoundrel with some of them. We begin to hallow his name by rejecting the fact that he sets us up, that he conditions us, that he programs us, that he manipulates us into becoming and being religious. He doesn't.

We begin to hallow God's name when we come to him with quiet childlike confidence, trusting him when he says (hear me now) trusting him when he says that he cares for each one of you, and for me, more than we can care for ourselves. Trusting him when he says that he loves us more than we can ever love ourselves. And trusting him, having confidence in him when he says that we can depend upon him more than we can ever depend upon ourselves or upon others.

You don't arrive at this confidence by argument or debate. You arrive at this confidence by accepting his self-revelation, his gift of himself to you this morning in Jesus Christ. He's giving himself to us in Jesus Christ, and in giving he evokes our confidence. Through Jesus Christ we have access to confidence. Confidence in God, confidence in ourselves, confidence in the world and the life we live. Think of those very briefly with me. Confidence in the world and the life we live through Jesus Christ. We can have it. Do you have it now?

Is this world a bit of cosmic debris? Did life occur by sheer random manner? Are we products of hydrogen, amino acids, and a chancy bit of lightning and nothing more? None of these questions can be answered by the whimsies of philosophy. People used to say that they could discover a *telos*, an end, a purpose in nature. And one man, Paley, said that this world was as if you suddenly became aware of the fact that you had found a watch in an open field, and you said this watch couldn't be ticking unless someone had manufactured it and wound it up. But that doesn't appeal to us, does it? In our modern day we are far more likely to listen to the astrophysicist, Fred Hoyle, from Cambridge University, England, the proponent of the "Big Bang" theory of the universe, when he tells us that in outer space there are myriads and myriads and myriads of organisms and that it is a sheer mathematical impossibility that you and I as we are known could have happened just randomly from these organisms. We begin to listen.

But the scientists' bafflement is not our source of confidence. Our confidence arises because we are startled by insight. As the Viennese-born physicist Victor Weiskopf once said, "The scientists, from time to time, are startled by insight." And do you know what startles us by insight? That when we talk about God we are talking about Jesus Christ the same yesterday, today and forever. Now, my dear friend, you can be confident in that kind of God.

And confidence in ourselves. Don't you find sometimes that your will seems to bend, and your capability to cope seems to yield in the face of what life asks of you? I think of the people to whom it has been our privilege to minister over several years here as we have shared together the struggles of life. We know that we don't have the answers within us, don't we?

And Peter knew it also—Peter who said, "Through him we have confidence in God." Who, Peter? "Through Jesus Christ, and I need to know about Jesus Christ," Peter would say, "because I'm brash and overconfident and my heart runs away with my head and my insight is swift sometimes but my performance is slow, and I go down to defeat in a big way, and my aggressiveness is just a cover-up for my cowardice. I need to know that I can be confident in someone." And that someone met this broken man on his way from an empty tomb after he had lied and denied and cursed that

God didn't matter for him. And that all right, if this prophet went to the gallows, so what? And when he met with this Jesus, he began to find a new confidence in himself growing deep in his heart.

And lastly, you not only can have confidence in this world and the life that we live in it and confidence in yourself because of Jesus Christ, you can have confidence in God. I'll tell it in the form of a story, if I may. My last story probably from this pulpit, but it illustrates what I want to say and of necessity, of course, it goes back to my native land, where I started. It was only a few years ago that Grace and I were on top of a huge rock which is known as the Orme, in Llandudno, the town from which we emigrated to the United States. People go to the top of the Orme to see the sunset in all its glory, the sun as a ball of fire descending behind scudding clouds, transforming an ocean into a myriad colors, and the moving clouds as if they were a kaleidoscopic evidence of beauty. They go up there and they weep at the beauty.

And as Grace and I were parked there a few years ago, taking all this glory in, a rather ramshackle car came next to us—ours wasn't too good, but this one was no better. And I looked out of the corner of my eye, and this is what I saw. I saw an older couple who obviously had had a child in their older years, and just as the sun as a ball of fire was descending into the gray ocean out there, they came around to the back door of the car and opened it and their son, now older, but obviously struck by a very incapacitating situation. I won't even try to describe it, but he couldn't move of his own accord. And I saw them tugging a little and bringing him to the edge of the seat so that his legs would hang over the seat. And he couldn't lift up his head, and just as the sun in all its magnificence was to give its final burst of glory, as if God were dazzling us by the pyrotechnics of his universe, they put their finger, the father did and the mother a little later, under this young man's chin and just pointed him out there.

And I knew at that moment, at that very moment I knew that God can dazzle us with all the magnificence of his universe, but that the secret of the universe is a love that comes to us in our frailty and our weakness and our need. It comes to us always asking our highest, but is never nearer to us than when we grope and sometimes grovel in the dust. I knew that the heart of the universe was revealing its glory, not in the sunset altogether, but in that compassion and grace and love which comes to us when we need it most and says there it is, there it is. And there, my boy, you are and you matter.

Don't try to take this world with its finitude of sin and suffering up to God and ask him for an explanation. Let us remember that he came down and still comes down to where we are day by day. He wants to accept us in our limitations, and he wants us to accept our limitations, to accept the fact that we're human, and to accept the fact that by all means there is no experience good or bad, right or wrong, in which he is not present. He's present in all of them to see us through, to enable us to be more than conquerors through Jesus Christ our Lord. Look up, look up; to this God I commend you, to this God, and I commend ourselves—the God and Father of our Lord Jesus Christ, to whom be all the praise and the glory, now and forever. Amen.

—May 6, 1984

Part Two

John M. Buchanan

Pastor, 1985–Present

JOHN McCORMICK BUCHANAN WAS BORN IN ALTOONA, Pennsylvania, and educated at Franklin and Marshall College and the Divinity School of the University of Chicago. He served two churches in Indiana before being called to the Broad Street Presbyterian Church in Columbus, Ohio, in 1974. Dr. Buchanan was installed as pastor of the Fourth Presbyterian Church in September 1985. He has been active in the Presbyterian Church (U.S.A.) at the presbytery, synod, and national levels, serving as moderator of the Committee on Review of the General Assembly Council at the 206th General Assembly in 1994. Dr. Buchanan and his wife Sue have five children and four grandchildren.

Sex, Scripture, and the Presbyterian Church

"You have heard that it was said. . . . But I say to you. . . ."

Matthew 5:27, 28 (NRSV)

I WAS TEMPTED TO PUT THE sermon title on the Michigan Avenue bulletin boards and see what might happen. I resisted the temptation because we have learned some things recently about what happens when the church tries to transact its business and conduct its conversations in public. It has been an interesting time to be a Presbyterian minister.

We have learned that there is more general interest in what the church has to say about sexuality than about any other topic—war, crime, drugs, race. We have, simply, never been in the news as much as we have recently, and the reason for that intense interest is itself a matter of major importance.

45

What the church thinks about and has to say about human sexual behavior is a matter of concern to a lot of people. Some feel very deeply about what the church should think and say. Many, many more are watching and listening carefully, and, I believe, openly hoping for a word which is relevant, timely, helpful, and faithful.

The topic itself is personal. Those of us who are talking about it today live on two sides of a major cultural revolution, an upheaval in public attitudes and behavior so huge that it is not unlike living in two different worlds. If you are my age or older, chances are you didn't talk about sex with your parents; sex education in public school meant a movie about venereal disease; your knowledge of human anatomy probably came from the Sears Catalog; couples kissed on screen and that's it; and there are words now used openly in casual conversation along Michigan Avenue which you did not hear said out loud, in mixed company, until you were in your thirties and which still cause you to flinch. If you live on the other side of the divide, your formative experience is very different. The only culture you know uses sex to sell beer and lawn mowers; sex before marriage is not only the statistical norm, but no one is much hiding it any longer. You know more and learned it earlier; and television, the dominant value shaper in your experience—not the church, your home or school—but television, has encouraged full sexual expression day-in and day-out all your lives. People my age used to hire a chaperone for a hayride and a housemother for the fraternity house. The raging moral debate today, say newspapers, is at what age it is appropriate to allow your teenage daughter's boyfriend to sleep over.

People who live on my side of the divide, and those who don't but wish they did, sometimes believe that the way to cope with the new world we are living in is to hold on for dear life to what we always assumed were absolutes. Curiously, our actual behavior didn't turn out to be much different from yours, but sometimes we're convinced that something critical to our culture's health, to the future's viability, our religion's existence, is lost unless we can hold on to those absolutes.

And into this fray comes the Presbyterian Church (U.S.A.) which two years ago appointed a task force to study and make recommendations on the topic of human sexuality. By the way, all of the major denominations are, or will be, dealing with these issues in the near future. The report was released and published several months ago, and it was acted on at the meeting of the church's General Assembly in Baltimore last week.

The report is two hundred pages long. To summarize it fairly would take hours. Most people made up their minds about its recommendation without even reading or seeing it. It says that we live in a patriarchal society and a patriarchal church, whose rules, morals, and traditions were formulated by men, for men. It says that patriarchal structures are not fair.

It says that the moral criterion for sexual relations is something it calls "justice-love," not marriage or gender or orientation alone. It says that "justice-love" is scriptural.

It also recommends that the Presbyterian family discuss these matters for two years and then make some changes in the way it talks publicly, and teaches its young, and ordains its leaders; that it include in its rite of ordination people who are now not included (namely "self-affirming, practicing homosexuals").

The report was controversial, divisive, and from the day it was published we have been discussing it in public. Some find it harsh and angry. Some think it is wonderful. Many conclude that its scholarship is ambitious and flawed and too political. Eighty-six of our presbyteries adopted overtures opposing the report before the General Assembly met. Our national offices in Louisville were inundated with thousands of letters. So many people ordered the report that it qualifies for a place on the *New York Times* bestseller list.

From across the country several national campaigns were organized, funded, and launched—a conservative organization solicited support and lobbied delegates to reject the report; liberal organizations advocated its adoption.

In the meantime, I sensed that a broad but silent spectrum of Presbyterians, and non-Presbyterians, had begun to take notice, to watch and listen for what the church had to say: Presbyterians who happen to be gay, lesbian Presbyterians, single young adult Presbyterians, Presbyterian college students, Presbyterian parents, Presbyterians with AIDS, Presbyterian parents and grandparents and aunts and uncles of persons with AIDS.

The Presbyterian Church is a family that operates on the basis of *Robert's Rules of Order*. In Baltimore the family gathered, first to talk about the matter and then to make some difficult but necessary decisions. And now I must tell you about the process, and it will be more than you wish to know. About an hour into the debate, the press became restless and some started to leave, eyes glazed over from substitute motions, amendments, amendments to amendments, points of order, calls for the question, and all done decently and in order and with general Presbyterian courtesy. About three hours into the debate, the friend with whom I was sitting, an executive with our board of pensions, turned to me and said, "Well, we've done it again. The church can even make sex boring."

First, the two-hundred-page report was examined, debated, and discussed by a standing committee made up of sixty-seven randomly selected commissioners. They held twelve hours of public hearings, listened to all the voices who wished to be heard, debated, argued, consulted with experts in medicine and psychiatry and church order, refined, discussed, and at 10:20 A.M. last Monday morning, brought the report to the floor of the Assembly Meeting in Baltimore's Convention Center, to a packed hall. The debate took all day.

The next morning the press announced, "Presbyterians Reject Report on Sex." That's not quite what happened. What the standing committee proposed and the Assembly did by a huge plurality was this. The Assembly decided to:

1. "Not adopt" the report on Human Sexuality, nor its recommendations, which is very different from rejecting it.

2. Dismiss the committee with thanks.

3. Request the Theology and Worship Unit to assist the church in exploring the significant biblical, theological, and ethical issues raised in the church around human sexuality during this past year and to use the Report, as well as a number of other documents, as resources. The essence of that proposal is that the congregation, where the family lives most intimately, is the best place for the conversation to continue.

4. And in a rare gesture it ordered a pastoral letter to be sent immediately to every Presbyterian church in the land.

The Session of Fourth Presbyterian Church acted on Friday to provide copies this morning. The letter addresses the following:

Our Presbyterian belief in Scripture as the authoritative word of God.

Our trust in the unconditional love of God for all persons.

Our affirmation that sexuality is a gift of God.

Our affirmation that the sanctity of the marriage covenant between one man and one woman is a God-given relationship to be lived out in fidelity.

An acknowledgement that the church still abides by its policies on ordination.

Finally, and this is a direct quote from the letter, "We reaffirm that the church is healthiest when it honors what we Presbyterians have always believed, as expressed in the 'Historic Principles' of 1788: That God alone is Lord of the conscience, and . . . that there are truths . . . with respect to which people of deep faith may differ. This is an opportunity to learn again what it means to be Presbyterian."

So, the conversation will continue, as it should. The Presbyterian Church did not reject the report but carefully, deliberately chose words to say what it means. It did "not adopt" the report. It referred the report to a process of continuing conversations where it will be one of several resources. The Church decided at this time not to change its policies on who is ordained, but to abide by existing policies while the conversation continues. The church rejected efforts from the right and the left to either draw the circle closer by condemning and rejecting or to eliminate the circle altogether. The middle held by very large pluralities. It is not always clear in the middle. But it is a very Presbyterian place to be.

Only a very brave or very foolish preacher would attempt to summarize what Scripture says about human sexuality in a single sermon. In fact, beware of sermons that claim to convey what the Bible says about sex. The Bible says a lot of different things and, as is often the case, it is possible to find a proof text for a number of different positions on every major behavioral question.

Jesus did not have a lot to say on the subject. Matthew, Mark, and Luke report that he said that a man who marries a divorced woman causes her to commit adultery. But almost all churches agree that this harsh position is not an absolute moral imperative, and that Jesus' high view of inviolable marriage was a radical and controversial departure from his own religious tradition which allowed a man to divorce a woman almost casually, and at one point mandated either divorce or polygamy if the woman did not bear children.

In the Hebrew Scriptures, sex outside of marriage is illegal—if the woman is married. It appears that the religious law is not much interested in sex between married men and unmarried women. Any sexual practice that does not propagate the race, increase the tribe, or that in any way threatens tribal culture is taboo. There are many prohibitions in the Old Testament, many of which were conditioned and shaped by the time, and many of which, we believe, have been superseded by the New Testament, although there is, and always has been, spirited debate about whether Jesus was interested in providing a new moral code to replace the old, or whether his message was a liberating gospel of forgiveness which puts the responsibility for making moral decisions squarely on each individual in each different situation.

Jesus didn't have much to say about sex. But one day, as he was teaching in the early morning, he was interrupted by the violent shouts of an unruly mob, dragging, pushing, shoving a woman right into the temple where he was sitting. There were two witnesses who said they had caught her in the act of sexual intercourse. The man had somehow escaped, but she, married, was guilty— adultery. The Scripture could not be more clear. She was to die, and the method of execution used in the first century was stoning.

It was a lynch mob and they were on their way to carry out the religiously mandated punishment. Why they stopped to talk with him no one knows. John suggests they hoped to catch him up, humiliate him. . . . "What are you going to do about this one,

Rabbi, caught in the act and you know as well as we what the law says? What does your love and acceptance say about adultery?"

And Jesus looked at them; so sure of themselves; so intent on preserving the morality of the community; so determined not to accommodate to the loose, secular permissiveness of Rome; so sure they knew the mind of God; and he looked at her, hysterical, terrified, moments away from an excruciating death, she who just a while ago was in the embrace of a man. Who knows why she did what she did: broke a basic moral law, decided to risk every-thing—her marriage, family, children, reputation, her life—for a moment of love. And then he did something strange. He bent and drew something in the dust. Again we don't know what. I believe he was thinking and that what he drew was just a tracing in the dirt while he was experiencing disgust at the self-righteousness of these religious men and anger at what religion, which begins with a loving God, can become, and revulsion at what was about to happen to a child of God. He straightened up, looked at them with what I imagine was a withering directness, and said, "Let the one without sin throw the first stone." And he went back to his tracing in the dust. One of the older men—wiser, a temple official—saw for a moment the truth of God in this peculiar rabbi and simply turned around and walked away. Another dropped the rock he still clutched in his hand and followed. And then another and another and another until they were all gone.

He looked up again at her, now alone, and I think, with a little sarcasm, maybe a twinkle in his eye, he said, "Where did they go? Has no one condemned you?" No sir. "Neither do I," he said. "Go your way—go back to your home—your children—your hus-band—your life—pick up the pieces. Don't do this again."

That moment is what the church is supposed to be. The sanc-tity of marriage is not demeaned by what he did, nor denied, but upheld. God's law is honored. Jesus does not condone adultery, but clearly his priority is life, not death, redemption, not rejection. Given an opportunity to say a clear word about morality, the word he chooses to say is mercy. It is a moment of grace and that's what his church should be: a place where above all and before all and after all we know about God's unconditional love and forgiveness and healing.

Church is the people, who when they gather weekly, praise God and then confess their sins, confess to the Creator and to one another that we are not perfect, not one of us; that we are sometimes intentional and sometimes unintentional sinners; that we live by grace and forgiveness and forbearance and love. And we confess it out loud so that God is not the only one hearing the truth about us, but our neighbors hear it also—hear that we know the truth about ourselves, that not one of us has the right to throw the first stone.

Church is where the stones start to drop from our hands as we learn compassion instead of condemnation, grace not judgment.

Church is where people who know who they are and who Jesus Christ is, take one another seriously and hear, with respect and love, the questions of teenagers about their sexuality (never asked directly of course); and with respect and compassion born of our mutuality in the grace of Christ, hear the dilemma of young adults, not married, but wondering if there is a word about faithfulness and integrity and responsibility; and the questions of homosexual people who did not choose to be who they are anymore than heterosexuals choose to be who they are, about what it means to be faithful and honest and responsible.

Church should be the refuge where the issues may be discussed in an atmosphere of respect, where each can look for guidelines—not rules—where the complexity of the world is appreciated and the freedom of the individual in the love of Christ is always affirmed.

At 5:30 P.M. last Monday, the General Assembly concluded the matter of the report on Human Sexuality. There was relief, a giddy sense that the body had not self-destructed, some laughter and even scattered applause. The moderator, Herb Valentine, a presbytery executive from Baltimore, an urban pastor I have known for twenty-five years, rapped the gavel. "There are brothers and sisters, sons and daughters who are in deep pain about what we have done," he said. "They are loyal Presbyterians. They are members and officers and ministers. They are gay and lesbian Presbyterians and their families. I have invited them to say their word and they have asked to say it silently and I have agreed. They wish to walk among us and I invite them and any who wish to walk with them to do so." The hall became absolutely silent. Three hundred people, gays, lesbians, their parents, men in jeans and T-shirts, and pin-stripes and button-down collars, women in slacks and power suits, people with AIDS. The person standing beside me pointed to a well-dressed, middle-aged man and woman holding hands, weeping openly, their recently dead. Some commissioners rose and joined the silent word. The three hundred fanned out and surrounded the commissioners' tables and sang quietly a song about acceptance and grace and freedom and the love of Jesus.

And so among us today, and every day, is a marvelous diversity of people, each one of us at a different place on our journey, some of us in deep pain, some of us in guilt, some of us wishing we were not who we are, some of us happy to be who we are, some of us struggling with our opinions and beliefs, not sure what we believe about these matters, all of us here because we trust a remarkable suggestion that God loves us, that we are children of God, that God's son does not condemn us, but offers forgiveness and healing and change and restoration and grace.

So this church, part of that Presbyterian family which lives under the authority of Scripture and also in dialogue with the world about us, lives by the grace of Jesus Christ, and will continue to be what it has been—a family of people who know who they are, who confess their sin together and celebrate the goodness of God's love, a place where all are welcome and included and affirmed and upheld, and respected and supported, as each struggles to find ways to live honestly and responsibly and faithfully.

—June 16, 1991

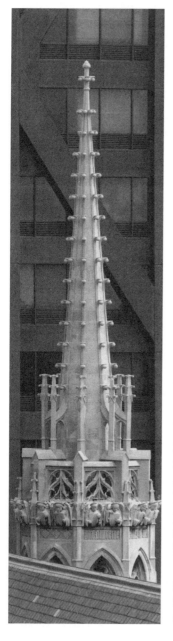

EIGHT

The City

As he came near and saw the city, he wept over it. . . .
Luke 19:41 (NRSV)

IT IS AN ANCIENT TRADITION OF the church that the palms which are given to churchgoers on Palm Sunday are saved for most of a year. In the homes of my friends who attended Catholic or Lutheran or some other fancy church, those palms were placed behind a picture frame in the sitting room where they became progressively more yellow and brittle. And then, according to custom, they are to be collected and burned. The ashes from the palms of Palm Sunday are then used to smudge a cross on the forehead of believers on Ash Wednesday.

The tradition is preserved and maintained by the Roman Catholic Church. We called over to Holy Name Cathedral this week and asked, and they said, "Yes, indeed; palms are burned and the ashes used on Ash Wednesday."

It's a good tradition. It's one of those eloquent gestures which we Protestants have left to the Roman Catholics, and we are the poorer for it. In fact, in one of the churches I served, we tried it on Ash Wednesday and a few Presbyterians found it meaningful; although I confess that I could not rid myself of the distinct sense that my militant Presbyterian Scotch-Irish grandmother was rolling her eyes in heaven and saying, "Really, now, is that necessary?"

It's a good tradition. We need the reminder—from palms to ashes to cross. The late William Stringfellow, an attorney who became one of the most articulate theologians of our era, used to worry a lot about Palm Sunday. We come to church on Palm Sunday, he used to say, because we love a parade. And we miss the power, the tragedy, and the drama. For Jesus, Stringfellow pointed out, it was a day of serious temptation and difficult decision. He was tempted when his friends and the crowd started treating him like royalty, waving palm branches, the symbol of Israel's patriotic aspiration, and chanting, "Blessed is the king who comes in the name of the Lord!"—which was the equivalent of the U.S. Marine Corps band playing "Ruffles and Flourishes," and "Hail to the Chief." When all that started to happen on the outskirts of the capital, Jesus, according to Stringfellow and many others, was authentically tempted to go for it, to claim the ancient throne of David, to rally the Zealots, put the hated Romans to the sword, and declare independence, reestablish the old monarchy.

And so when the city comes into view for the first time on the road down from the Mount of Olives, and Jesus stops the procession, looks at the city, its wall and rooftops reflecting the morning sun, what he doesn't say is stunning.

He weeps. This is not eyes moistening slightly. This is real weeping. This is a lament which the biblical scholars define "a voice of love and profound caring, a vision of what could have been and of grief over its loss of personal responsibility and frustration, of sorrow and anger mixed" (Fred Craddock, *Luke* in Interpretation series [Westminster/John Knox, 1990], 229).

So in this moment, it is Jesus powerfully expressing love and hope and grief and letting go of perhaps his greatest temptation, to take control and lead the nation—the city. It is Jesus, choosing love and service and sacrifice over power and control and authority.

And he says: "If you only know the things that make for peace. But they are hidden from your eyes. The day will come when your enemies will crush you." And that, of course, is what happened. At least four decades elapsed between this day and Luke writing it down. And by the time Luke wrote, there had been a number of armed insurrections until in A.D. 70 the Romans had enough of it, devastated the city, leveled the temple, and dispersed the Jews. So in a terribly historical way, Jesus was exactly right when he said amidst his weeping that the city was blind.

And then, of course, he went straight to the temple and what he did then was very significant. He didn't say prayers or make a sacrifice; he became angry at the corruption of the sacrificial system, and he physically ejected the profiteers; and then he sat down to teach and heal and listen and encourage all the sorts of people who ordinarily weren't in the temple. It was an act, most agree, that guaranteed his execution (*see* John Dominic Crossan, *The Historical Jesus*, [HarperSanFrancisco, 1992], xii).

There is much more going on here than the parade. Frederick Buechner reflects:

> He looked at the city and wept. . . . The palm branches. The hosannas. Triumph and hope and healing were what the shouting was about that day, and if Palm Sunday services are any more than ecclesiastical jamborees, liturgical vaudeville, then it's because some echo of that shouting is with us still. (*A Room Called Remember*, [Haper & Row, 1984], 74)

There is much more going on here than the parade. There is first of all, the simple fact that he came to the city. I discovered an absolutely delightful detail in a new and highly regarded book by DePaul's John Dominic Crossan, distinguished scholar. Crossan says there was a superstition among the rural peasants of Galilee in the first century that "the most powerful demons are not found in small villages but in certain cities." Professor Crossan suggests that when Jesus exorcised a demon, the people might have concluded that the demon headed for Jerusalem (Crossan, xi).

Not a bad metaphor, actually. I know people who think like that. In fact the thought occurs to me—as I ponder a rush-hour trip to O'Hare—that some very real demons have found their way to the city recently.

He came to the city. He wept because the city was blind, and to observe this day with integrity is to ask what it is we see when we look at the city; or to shift the image slightly, what it is we hear when we turn our ear to our city.

The Chicago Symphony Orchestra, I hope! And the Lyric Opera and Music of the Baroque, the blues and jazz at Andy's, "Take Me Out to the Ball Game" at the seventh-inning stretch, and the Fourth Presbyterian Church Morning Choir. But there are other voices; voices which, if you have the courage to hear, will make you weep.

Pharoah and Lafeyette Rivers, for instance, the boys in Alex Kotlowitz's *There Are No Children Here* [Doubleday, 1991], go about life in a Chicago public-housing project. Their friend Bird Leg, fifteen, is dead, shot on a playground on a hot August night by a rival gang member. Pharoah and Lafeyette attended the funeral with their family.

> As the boys waited to file out of their aisle, they heard a mother, two rows back, scold her son, "That could have been you if I'd let you go over there. . . ."
>
> "We're gonna die one way or the other by killing or plain out," James said to Lafeyette. "I just wanna die plain out."
>
> Lafeyette nodded. "Me too." (p. 51)

Or hear the voice of Nikkeye, who is seventeen and lives in Camden, New Jersey, and has been a prostitute since she was thirteen. *Time* featured Camden in its January 20, 1992, issue in an article entitled "Who Could Live Here?" Camden, a once-thriving industrial center is a gutted, flattened city of one hundred thousand, half under twenty-one, with two hundred liquor stores and no theaters, where you can buy a hand grenade for four hundred dollars on the street and where infants die at twice the national average, which means at Third World rate or worse. Nikkeye told *Time*:

> "I been stabbed, raped, stomped, kidnapped and beaten up. The only thing that's never happened to me is—I never died. I figure I know everything there is to know. I probably know more than the President. I don't know how to ride a bike. I've never been to a zoo."

Or hear the voice of Rev. Johnny Ray Youngblood, pastor of St. Paul Community Baptist Church, Brooklyn, at the funeral of Ian Moon, one of the two young men shot and killed in the hallway of their high school. Mr. Youngblood's eulogy, which was reprinted on the editorial page of the *New York Times*, quoted Mayor Dinkins:

> "The Mayor said something that shook me," the minister remarked. "He said Ian has gone to be with God. That's frightening because if Ian is with God, what is he going to tell God about us when he gets there?"

The first thing and perhaps the most important thing about this day is that Jesus came to the city and loved it enough to know its promise, and enough to hope for its future, and loved it enough to weep over it. And so, I have trouble observing this day without looking and listening to the city, our American cities, this city. It seems to me, that it's the least we can do—to thrill at the glory of the place, its beauty, its strength, its grace and its hope, and, if necessary, to weep at its despair and tragedy.

There is in this city a lethal combination of forces which is creating an urban problem so large we can no longer even see the entire picture. Poverty—drugs—violence. Public housing—crack—guns—despair—gangs—assault rifles. And beneath it all, what appears for all the world like a massive, unconditional political surrender, the federal government hands urban problems to the state. The state is broke and hands them on to the city itself. At all three levels people get elected by promising to cut spending and never raise taxes, looking at the private sector which responds with some justification that its primary business is business, commerce, not urban violence, education, and health care, which leaves the churches. We have refused to think in new ways about drugs and gangs and guns. But there are not enough police, not enough courtrooms, not enough jails to begin to win the vaunted war we declared and have already lost. Because of poverty—despair—and drugs, an enterprising child in Cabrini-Green [public housing project] will look out at the world and make some basic decisions. In Camden, *Time* said, and it is true here, "An eight-year-old 'watcher' on a bicycle, keeping a look out for police, earns fifty dollars a day. A twelve year old can earn twice that much making a few deliveries; a carrier earns four hundred dollars for the trip to the next major city."

And so on the day our Lord wept over the blindness of the city, the least we can do is make sure that we see what has become of us.

And homelessness. Dr. Lewis Thomas, former head of the Sloane Kettering Cancer Clinic and popular author, wrote that "a society can be judged by the way it treats its most disadvantaged, its least beloved, its mad. As things now stand, we must be judged a poor lot, and it is time to mend our ways" (*Late Night Thoughts in Listening to Mahler's Ninth Symphony*, [Viking Press, 1983], 100).

On April 1, the *Tribune* said bluntly, "Today marks a moral low point for Illinois government. Forty thousand of the state's most destitute people are being cut loose from the smallest, most basic form of public assistance."

We could, of course, do it better. We could be better. We could be a city that cares for its least, that shelters its homeless, that tends to its sick, and educates its children. But it will require a new way of thinking. And it will require sacrifice and money; and if we know anything from our own pathetic history, it is that there are no quick fixes, including turning this beautiful city into the gambling capital of the Mid-west. It's not just the tragedy and pathos and crime and prostitution and ugliness which follows it wherever it goes, regardless of what the experts testify. It is that, of course, but what is reason to weep today is the suggestion that we have a way to fix our city which will not cost us anything, will require no sacrifice at all—other than the sacrifices of those who play, 60 percent of whom are always, everywhere, the poor.

So today, may we who come here to observe the parade see the city and hear the city and, if need be, weep for the city.

And the other thing about this day is that by coming to the city, Jesus showed where religion is to be focused. Last week I attended a forum on "Faith and Work," how a personal religious faith affects the worlds of work and politics and leisure and family. The results of a recent survey were shared and discussed. For most people in the mainline churches, religious faith affects family life, but has very little to do with either their work or politics or their leisure. Chicago Theological Seminary scholar Susan Thistlethwaite observed that Christians have not always agreed that religion ought to have political, social, or vocational impact. There has always been, she said, a suspicion among sectarians that when faith and politics, faith and the world of work meet, faith is diluted.

Professor Glenn Tinder wrote about *The Political Meaning of Christianity* and observed similarly that we want to keep spirituality separate from the more complex areas of our lives. And he concludes that there is a very basic theological error in that. On this day we celebrate our Lord's coming to the city—not the retreat center, monastery, cloister, but the noisy, wonderful, tragic, glorious heart of the city. We celebrate his coming to the temple and turning it around and opening its door to the poor, sick, blind, outcast.

Somewhere in each of us, I suppose, is a wish that he hadn't done that; a desire to keep our God safely transcendent, to keep our Lord in the pleasant, rolling hills of Galilee, keep our own religion confined to the church sanctuary on Sunday morning. And that might be a tenable position to assume—except for the fact that he rode into the city.

In that sense, it's bad news, I suppose. But, as is often the case with religion, it is also the good news because it means that God's commitment to us is absolute, and God's coming into the center of our lives is relentless and determined and strong. There is on that road down from the Mount of Olives not only despair but great hope—the desperate shouts of an oppressed people, but also the hosannas of those who are sustained by hope in God which is always, at the same time, hope for the future. There is in his weeping both grief and also deep love for the city. And there is in the whole gesture, the whole panorama of this day, a promise that Jesus Christ comes to the city, our city—redemptively, decisively, creatively, hopefully—and to your heart and mine.

His love for and commitment to the human city includes you and me in our individuality and privateness. He comes to meet us, to listen to us, to receive our hosannas, to teach us—but also to forgive us, to heal us, and to accept us in places we thought ourselves to be unacceptable and in ways we thought were impossible.

He comes—where you live and move and have your being—to be your Lord, your Savior, your friend—in your heart of hearts, where you love and hope and dream, where you store the memories of your failures and betrayals and your victories and highest joys. He comes to the city.

Did you notice, as I did for the first time actually, the words his disciples chant along the road: "Blessed is the king. . . . Peace in heaven, and glory in the highest heaven!"

Those words are strikingly similar to words the angels sang at his birth. "Glory to God in the highest heaven and on earth peace."

That's what this day is about. It is what he is about. And it is what we must be about now.

Glory to God among us, riding on a donkey. Glory to God for showing us how to love. Glory to him who showed us how to live courageously and die faithfully. And peace—here—in this city—in your heart and mine.

"Blessed is the king who comes in the name of the Lord!"

—April 12, 1991

NINE

Christian Common Sense about Politics

"Give to the emperor the things that are the emperor's, and to God the things that are God's."
Mark 12:17 (NRSV)

I LOVE THE FOURTH OF JULY. I love the simplicity and integrity of parades, fireworks, picnics. One of the best pieces on patriotism I ever read was written by the late Joseph Sittler, professor of theology at the University of Chicago. Sittler said:

> Before the word America can set one thinking or planning or resolving or defending, it ought to set one dreaming and remembering. And out of this dreamed procession of America as a concrete place will be poured the ingot of a tough and true patriotism. (*Grace Notes and Other Fragments*, [Fortress Press, 1981], 101)

I love the Fourth of July because it is an opportunity to remember and dream:

62

Remember what this nation, this lively and fragile experiment is about, and dream about what it could be for generations to come. And for people of faith, it is an opportunity—an obligation, I actually believe—to reflect on the relationship between our faith commitments and our commitment to the public, or political arena.

The best way to celebrate the Fourth of July, I have been told, is to return to the U.S.A. from a trip abroad. This year I learned the truth of that advice. Some of us returned on Friday at the end of twelve days in Italy, a good portion of which was spent, in one way or another, thinking about the historic connections and disconnections between our religion and the political state. Members of the Morning Choir and twenty church members traveled to Rome and Florence; the choir sang three wonderful concerts to very appreciative audiences. Last Sunday morning the choir sang, and we all attended worship, at the Waldensian Church in Rome. The Waldensians are Italian Protestants who are part of the Reformed Presbyterian family.

The topic was set for me by one of the first things we saw as soon as we arrived in Rome, the cell where tradition says St. Paul was held before his martyrdom by Rome. There is, of course, no historical verification, but whether or not he was held in that spot and executed in the place the tour guide explains, no one much disputes the notion that he was in prison and along with thousands of others, branded a traitor by the political authorities, arrested, tortured, and executed.

It was a sobering reminder that at the beginning we learned to be leery of the state. Christians in Rome, for fear of being exposed and identified, dug tunnels underground to bury their own dead, and then used those same tunnels, the Catacombs, for worship and socialization.

But it was no more sobering for me, at least, than the visible reminder of what happens when the state adopts Christianity, incorporates it, sponsors it. The emperor Constantine, in 303, legalized Christianity and before long Christianity was the official religion of Rome, and for sixteen hundred years the church acted like God's government on earth. In a recent essay on the Church in the Third Millennium, theologian Juergen Moltmann observes that for more than a thousand years, the church, "Instead of spreading the Gospel of Christianity in order to awaken faith, spread the Kingdom of Christ in order to rule in God's name" (*Theology Today*, April, 1994).

One day Jesus dealt with it. It's near the end of the story when the conflict between him and the religious and political authorities has deepened. A group of critics has come to contend with him, perhaps even discredit him in the eyes of his increasingly zealous followers. They ask a question for which there is no good answer: "Is it lawful to pay taxes to the emperor?" The tax in question is the head tax, a hated reminder that the real authority in Israel is Caesar. However he answers, he's going to be in trouble. The Zealots, a fanatically nationalistic political organization, of which Judas Iscariot may have been a member, held that the tax was illegal and should not be paid as a gesture of civil disobedience. Many people secretly admired them and their brave protests against Roman authority.

If Jesus said, "Pay the tax; it is legitimate," he would, in fact, have discredited himself with many people as a Roman collaborator. On the other hand, if he took the Zealot position and advised not paying the tax, he would have been arrested on the spot for sedition.

His response, in that circumstance, is subtle and remarkable: "Let me see a coin," he says. The image of Caesar was on the coin—it was Caesar's money, government money. "Give it to him," Jesus says; "it's his anyhow. Give to God what is God's."

A simplistic way to interpret his answer is that there is no connection between religious faithfulness and the political arena. And it seems, at first, as if that is exactly what he means. Religion and politics are completely distinct. Keep them altogether separate. Be an obedient citizen and a faithful Christian in separate ways. It has been a popular notion within Western Christianity: two realms— "the City of God and the City of Man"—with no relationship between them. It was the theological rationale behind the ability of some Christians in Nazi Germany to work in the death camps all week and go to church on Sunday.

That total separation of religion from politics would have been surprising to Jesus. Actually, he is teaching one of Israel's oldest and most precious creeds, the sovereignty of God. Actually, it is a sarcastic answer, and his hearers probably got it. Caesar is thrown a crumb. "Here . . . look at his picture . . . give him what he has coming. The Lord God, the sovereign and only King of all creations, owns everything. You owe everything to God: everything you have, everything you are."

The ones who have come to discredit him are astonished. It's not the answer they wanted. God is Lord of all: all individuals, all nations, emperors, and empires; God is sovereign even over religious institutions. It is an amazing answer. It describes an active engagement of faithful people in the political process, but it is very clear about where ultimate sovereignty or authority lies.

It is not an easy lesson to learn. Our Old Testament lesson this morning is one of our oldest stories, from a time when God's people had not yet made the transition from a federation of tribes, recently settled down after wandering around the desert, to a nation, with institutions to maintain and borders to secure and policies to establish. Prophets, priests, and judges have been political structures enough for the tribes of Israel, but now they want to be like other nations. "Give us a king," they say to Samuel, their prophet and leader. And Samuel, with wit and eloquence, tells them about the ways of a king.

"He'll draft your son for the army; he'll appropriate your farms; he'll take your daughters for his household; he'll take a tenth of your grain, and your cattle and donkeys. Sooner or later, you'll think your purpose is to provide for the comfort and well being of the king."

Samuel is very leery of concentrated political power. His warning to the children of Israel was the text of many a diatribe against our own government in the sixties.

Interestingly, God is not quite as grim about the political prospects as Samuel. "Listen to the people," God tells Samuel. "Give them a king." God is a realist. After all, there aren't any good alternatives. God sounds like Winston Churchill who, in a debate about the strengths and weaknesses of democracy, admitted that democracy is full of weaknesses, inefficiencies, but every other system of government is worse. Israel has to start acting like a nation in order to survive. But there is a wistfulness to it, almost as if God knows people are always going to have trouble with this and furthermore that the ones who become king, the political authorities, are always going to have trouble acknowledging their own limits. God knows, apparently, that the temptation is always for the king or queen—the state, if you will—to think that is it God.

Give to Caesar what is Caesar's and to God what is God's. The earliest Christian creed was "Jesus Christ is Lord," and in the days of high Roman imperialism, it was a political statement. What it meant was "The emperor is not Lord. The state is not Lord." And in that simple affirmation, Christianity deprived the emperor, and every totalitarianism in history, from Nero to Hitler, to failed Marxist regimes in Poland, Czechoslovakia, Hungary, the Soviet Union, of the one thing totalitarianism must have, and that is the unquestioned loyalty and obedience of its subjects. "Jesus Christ is my Lord" was first of all a political statement. And people who said it were not scolded for their misguided theology. They were executed for treason.

One of the most important and most precious tenets of Christian faith, as we Presbyterians see it, is the sovereignty of God and therefore the limitations on the sovereignty of any human authority, king, government, or church. "God alone is Lord of the conscience," we like to say, and by that we mean that there is about you and me something which we owe to no one but God and furthermore that good government understands that about itself.

The glory of this experiment is precisely its idea of the limitations of government when it comes to matters of conscience and faith and its protection of the liberty of all its citizens to follow the dictates of their own conscience.

We're different in this respect. Leslie Gelb wrote an editorial in the *New York Times* a while ago in which he observed that most of the nations of the world are organized on some principle of exclusion: race, religion, language, ethnicity. And with frightening violence, exclusive groups are willing to go to war with other groups to protect their own exclusiveness.

I don't travel a lot, but every time I am out of the country, I understand more clearly how unique and precious this experiment is. We are different here. This is for all of us. This means to include us all. A friend of mine works for the Chicago Stock Exchange and spends a lot of time traveling in the Third World.

He is an African American, and I assume that he knows something about racial exclusiveness. My assumption is that it has not been easy for him in the world of banking. Recently, I heard him make a speech and say, "I'm a liberal and there's a lot about what's going on that I don't like, but I love this country. I travel a lot and I see the lines of people at our embassies all over the world trying to get in. Why? Because they've heard about freedom and opportunity and chance here: that everybody is included."

Cornell West, head of the department of African American studies at Princeton, said in a speech recently that the loss of that sense of community, the inclusive community, is our greatest danger. "Two hundred and eighteen years after the beginning of this precious democratic project, democracy is fragile . . . this notion that we are all in this together, that if the ship springs a leak, we are all going to drown."

West and other historians note that the founders of the Republic, even though they did not include the people who were brought here as slaves, nevertheless put in place a system that acknowledges the public arena, the common good. It's in the Preamble to the Constitution.

> We the people of the United States, in order to form a more perfect union, establish justice, insure domestic tranquility, provide for the common defense, promote the general welfare, and secure the blessings of liberty for ourselves and our posterity, do order and establish this Constitution. . . .

"The common welfare." It's for all of us, not just those of us who came from Northern Europe, but those who came from Asia, and Southern Europe, and Africa, and South America, and those who were already here and who have the only really legitimate claim on the land.

Cornell West is one of a growing number of thoughtful critics who suggest that the radical and romanticized individualism which is such an integral part of how Americans see themselves may prove to be our most vulnerable characteristic, and our most serious weakness. Consider the unprecedented violence that threatens to destroy our cities. What else can one make of a country where children carry handguns to schools, where murder is the leading cause of death for African American males, where we seem determined in the name of individual freedom to not be satisfied until each one of us is armed against all the rest of us? No other country in the world thinks like that—that "Dodge City privatization of security," West says.

As we head toward the end of the century, we need a renewed sense of the public good, the general welfare. We Christians particularly need to take our stand for a nation and a culture which is truly inclusive, where no one is excluded by reason of race, religion, ethnicity. And we need to make our voice heard a little more clearly when the name "Christian" is misappropriated by any coalition, any church, that claims God's truth, God's will is its own private property.

We need to stop shouting slogans at one another and learn again the gift of public discourse, expressing differences of opinion about important matters without calling into question the political loyalty or religious orthodoxy of others.

Analysts of the left and the right, liberals and conservatives, lament the spiritual impoverishment of our nation at this point in its history, the loss of meaning and hope, the absence of a vision of the nation's purpose and destiny. From all sides of the political spectrum comes a new awareness that a culture driven apparently only by its market, and the market values it spawns, is a poor culture ultimately; and if history is any teacher, a culture destined to either collapse or to spin apart into small, rigidly structured self-interested and self-absorbed segments.

So may I presume to suggest that our fundamental need in these times is to recover the truly traditional values which do have their roots in the Judeo-Christian tradition at its best, its most liberal and open and inclusive?

May I suggest to you that we cannot and should not try to go back to a vision of our nation as an extension of Great Britain, white and Christian. But instead, in the name of the God of the whole creation, who created human beings in many colors, embrace with faith and eagerness the gorgeous pluralism which tries to exist here?

And may I suggest that it is our religious duty to welcome customs and mores of others, even when to do so means limiting our right to practice our own publicly?

And may I suggest that among our most precious values is a sense of the community, the public, the whole people, and that when all the people do not have access to the best the culture produces—health care, education, public safety, housing, transportation, and opportunity—by reason of economics, race, or political intent, it is our sacred duty to change the system and to do better. And that it is the only way we will survive?

And we should, I presume to suggest, give God thanks for the precious experiment that in spite of its lapses, its occasional forgetfulness about its own most precious traditions, still intends to include all of God's children and to hold up to the world a picture of what human life under God's sovereignty might look like.

And may I suggest finally that not only did our Lord Jesus not suggest a separation of religion and politics, but quite the opposite, quite radically so? May I suggest that public political involvement is our sacred duty; that he calls us to give Caesar his due in the context of God's sovereignty, the God of all people, all nations, all races . . . the God to whom we owe everything . . . and whom to serve is both our sacred duty and highest joy?

—July 3, 1994

TEN

Who Wants to Be Number One?

". . . Whoever wishes to become great among you must be your servant."

Mark 10:43 (NRSV)

WE HAVE HEARD IT SO OFTEN that we no longer experience its power. In fact, I wonder if we ever truly hear it: "Whoever wishes to become great among you must be your servant, and whoever wishes to be first among you must be slave to all."

It's in the text for the day and just about the time I was starting to think about it, and how church folk have heard so many attempts to interpret it and apply it with energy and imagination, just about the time I was about to set aside this overused and worn-out saying of Jesus in favor of something a little livelier and more interesting, I heard from Emilie Beck, a member of this congregation. She is a nurse, and a few months ago, when the newspapers and television news shows and national magazines were full of those ghastly pictures from Rwanda, the brutal violence, the starvation, the suffering simply beyond our capacity to comprehend, Emilie got it in her mind that she ought to do something. So she did some quick research and discovered a volunteer ecumenical organization of health-care professionals who had access to the refugee camps and some of the worst situations of human suffering; and in the middle of the summer, just as I was getting ready to go to the ocean for a week, Emilie finished up her inoculations and flew to Rwanda. Her letter arrived two weeks ago.

> Hello from Kigali—where my hardy band of evangelicals and I have started up Central Kigali Hospital, once 600 beds, from scratch. This torn, bullet-pockmarked, and mortar-destroyed city once had a population of 350,000, but the U.N. reports that 80,000 have died following a machete massacre. I have seen the evidence. [There follow several paragraphs of details, too brutal to speak about.]
>
> At first, I worked in the adult cholera wards until it was discovered that I had pediatric experience and was assigned the unenviable task of opening the pediatric ward. Being Presbyterian, I approached the task similarly to how I thought Florence Nightingale would, insisting on a much higher degree of cleanliness and sanitation than would be thought, seeing that we had no electricity or running water.
>
> My team of Rwandans—nurses, translators, cleaners—are simply superb and we have a census of at least twenty children— at least two of whom die at night, sometimes three or four.

And then she explains how sometimes the babies die in her arms: "Sometimes children die so suddenly and swiftly it seems as if they 'evaporate' and I am left peering into a shaft of light that weakly penetrates fixed, dilated pupils, a sign of irreversible brain damage. I don't even do CPR anymore, for there is nothing to bring them back to." [Letter used by permission.]

She finished the letter from Nairobi where she had been sent for some rest. She tells us about worshiping in a Pentecostal church because the Presbyterian church in Rwanda was blown to bits. "You don't know how lucky you are in America. Keep praying," she urges us, "and thank you for your support, especially Nancy, who thought this was a calling. Fondly, Emilie."

Well, according to Jesus, Emilie is the greatest. She is first among all of us—or at least in the first rank of those who serve—humbly, quietly, helpfully: our great ones. It is, in fact, a calling—a direct and specific one at that. It is what Jesus told his disciples to do.

The incident happens three times in Mark's Gospel. On the way to Jerusalem, Jesus warns his disciples that the road ahead will not be easy—that he's headed for a confrontation with the authorities and the results will not be pleasant. In all probability he will suffer; in all probability he will not survive.

And three times the disciples don't hear, or refuse to hear. First it's Peter: "God forbid, Lord, that anything like that should happen to you."

The second time, he warns them about the suffering ahead; and this time they're arguing about who among them is the greatest. It's very bad taste to say the least. He's talking about his death, and they're arguing about rank and privilege.

A third time it happens: the warning about suffering and death. This time it's James and John, part of the inner circle, his closest friends, who choose the moment to present an almost infantile request: "Teacher, we want you to do for us whatever we ask."

Well, who wouldn't? "Do me a favor?" we ask. I always want to say, "Before I answer that, tell what the favor is." Their request is outrageous: "Let us sit at your right hand and left hand in your glory."

He's walking toward his death and they're still assuming that he'll become king and they'll reap the rewards of association with him. They hear the words but not the music, someone quipped. Jesus is leading, but they're headed in the opposite direction.

And then, to make matters worse, the other ten get angry with them—not, one suspects, because they have been so thoughtlessly tasteless, but because James and John beat everybody else to the punch. Each of them had wanted to make that request for privilege, prestige, position—greatness.

His response, given the conditions, is extraordinary. He doesn't criticize or scold them for their lack of sensitivity. He doesn't tell them it's wrong to be thinking like that at a time like this. What he says is that you've got the basics all wrong. Sitting at the right and left hand of the King is not greatness—at least in God's eyes. Greatness is service. If you want to be first, you have to be last. If you aspire to greatness, you have to learn about service.

That is a radically different agenda from the one they assumed was operating. And behind it is a radically different social vision from their society's, and our own for that matter. They knew what greatness meant. Caesar was great. Herod was great. Great men have power. They have people around them catering to their every whim. A great man isn't a servant—he has servants. And so it is: Greatness is a state measured by dollars, firepower, horsepower. Greatness is having enough to never have to serve anyone.

Novelist and social critic Tom Wolfe continues to look deeply into the heart of our culture. In his novel, *Bonfire of the Vanities* [Farrar, Straus, Giroux, 1987], the 1980s' obsession with money and easy equation of wealth with greatness is portrayed with unblinking accuracy and brilliant sarcasm, something the motion picture never quite captured. The main character, Sherman McCoy, an enormously successful bond salesman, gets in a lot of trouble, personally and financially. Things are going from bad to worse, but he's in a kind of solid gold trap. Wolfe writes about him:

> Obviously he could cut down . . . but not nearly enough. There was no getting out from under the $1.8 million loan, the crushing $21,000-a-month note, without paying it off or selling the apartment and moving into one far smaller, and more modest—an impossibility! Once you had lived in a $2.6 million apartment on Park Avenue—it was impossible to live in a $1 million apartment. Obviously, there was no way to explain this to a living soul. [pp. 137–38]

Greatness is military power—or professional excellence. Greatness is being the biggest and best. Greatness is being number one, which is such a cultural icon with us that little-league athletes celebrate their every success with our most visible symbol—one raised finger, thrust into the air—"We're number one!" One hastens to add that it has not been much of a temptation recently for admirers of the Cubs.

Jesus turned upside down the definition of religion in his world. One of the observations of current scholarship on the life and times of Jesus is that he challenged the very foundation of religion and life in general by redefining the purpose of religion as compassion, mercy, kindness, service, love of neighbor; instead of moral purity, cleanness, holiness, obedience to the rules and regulations that defined religious orthodoxy. According to Marcus Borg, a professor of religion at Oregon State University, who has written a new book, *Meeting Jesus Again for the First Time* [HarperSanFrancisco, 1994], Jesus' radical contribution to religious thought is his idea of God as compassionate instead of holy; God as merciful and kind, instead of transcendent and other; God as nurturing and embracing, rather than God in a remote part of the heavens holding court and judging the moral and political shortcomings of human beings. It was his radical theology, Borg says, that led him to challenge his culture's basic assumptions. Because God was compassionate, God's people—politically and socially—should be guided more by compassion than by a desire to be pure. And religion—the religion of Jesus—was very different from his people's or any people's religion. It produced an open, inclusive, accepting community of people who were far more worried about not excluding anyone than they were about maintaining appropriate boundaries to keep the righteous in and the sinners out.

For Jesus, what mattered most was compassion and its behavioral expression in service. Thus, he was perfectly serious when he said that people who strive for greatness must learn to serve.

Let's go in deeper. If Jesus was right about God; if God is compassionate, and if we are created in the image of God, then being compassionate and serving others is simply being who we were created to be, being fully human, listening to our deepest instincts.

Robert Coles, a psychiatrist who teaches at Harvard, thinks you can see that in us if you observe carefully. He describes a scene many of us have witnessed: sleeping babies in a nursery, quietly dozing. One of the babies starts crying, in pain, or colic, and the other babies respond with their cries. But, says Coles, who is a child psychiatrist and knows about these things: "Their cries are not the cry of pain but rather the cry of empathy in response to someone else's pain. These children are not even old enough to have language but they respond instinctively to someone else's cry." Concludes Dr. Coles, "You're in the presence of the child's first responses to the outside world" (*Homiletics*, vol. 6, no. 3]).

William Bennett, in his current bestseller, *The Book of Virtues* [Simon & Schuster, 1993], includes compassion and also refers to the nursery:

> It is our twentieth-century understanding that human infants do not distinguish between their own distress and that of others. One baby's cries in the nursery are frequently picked up by the rest, and together they form a natural choral symphony of sympathetic woe. (p. 1,070)

Not only are we at our most human and our best when we serve others, we also invariably learn something important, namely that the one who benefits most from acts of service is the one who does the serving. One of the closely guarded secrets of ministry is that people think that we are doing them a favor and thank us profusely for visiting them in the hospital, or in retirement homes—but ministers all know and experience that the benefit ultimately is ours.

Robert Coles has written a book, *The Call of Service* [Houghton Mifflin, 1993], in which he tells a charming story about nine-year-old Ruth Ann, a fourth-grade student in a ghetto school where Coles does his service as a teacher. With childish candor, Ruth Ann asks him, "We were wondering why you come over here . . . [you] must be pretty busy . . . where did you get the idea, did you hear something bad about us?" And then she tells Coles about overhearing her mother good-naturedly complain about all the volunteers who come into the housing project and how she has to take them by the hand to orient them and sometimes protect them. Nine-year-old Ruth Ann said to Dr. Coles, "It's nice that some of you folks come here . . . and we'll try [to help you,] to tell you everything we know" (p. xvii).

Robert Coles, psychiatrist, knows that sometimes the healthiest, most therapeutic prescription he makes is suggesting to troubled people that they find someone else to worry about and care for and serve. He reflects: "The call of service [is] a call toward others . . . but also a call inward, a call to oneself" (p. 284). "Whoever wishes to be great must be your servant and whoever wishes to be first— must be slave of all." Jesus' words come as a jolt to self-centered religion which focuses exclusively on personal salvation, personal moral purity and theological orthodoxy. His words come as a challenge to churches whose purpose is institutional maintenance or survival. The Church of Jesus Christ is a service institution. Sometimes we're asked why we place such a premium on our community ministries; why we talk so much about tutoring and counseling and social services and housing and clothing; why we are always talking about other people instead of us; why we insist on investing our resources in programs for others.

This is the answer. It's what Jesus, Lord of the Church, told us to do. It's what we're here for. And no, it isn't going to solve the mammoth urban problems of housing, employment, racism, education—which conspire against brothers and sisters who are, literally, our neighbors. We are not naive. It is not enough. It is not even very much. But it is what our Lord told us to do—to try to be great, not by the size of our budget or the elegance of our building, but by the service we perform.

We do it as a church, a community which lives in the midst of the most exuberantly materialistic segment of our culture, arguably one of the glitziest intersections in America, precisely because it is so important to hold up an alternate social vision here, a vision of a society in which people care most of all about one another. We do it precisely because each of us cannot go to Rwanda, or build a house or serve a meal or teach a child, but some of us can, and will, and do, on behalf of all of us. In a very real sense which she, I know, understands, Emilie is in Kigali because we are here and she is there for us. And so is each tutor, each volunteer.

Why do we spend so much energy and resources on others? Well, if truth be known, there is a sense in which we don't. We may not plan it that way—but the benefit is ours. We do it because our Lord has shown us that it is how we become fully human, God's children, crowned with glory and honor. It's his prescription for our greatness.

Not all of us can serve as tutors. But some can. Not many of us can go to Rwanda. But one did. Each of us, however, can be a servant. And I know many, many who are servants with grace, and anonymity, and courage and compassion: giving time, resources, little bits of life, energy, hope, skills, love, sometimes pouring out life; serving—feeding the homeless; or feeding an aging parent; tutoring a youngster; or attending to the urgent needs of her own twelve-year-old son or grandson who is an innocent victim of a world characterized by gangs, drugs, guns; building a house with Habitat or simply refusing to abandon a home in which there lives a difficult spouse. I know, and so do you, great servants who quietly tend to people around them— their husbands, wives, their parents, children, their partner dying of AIDS. I know many humble and anonymous servants who do God's work, who follow Jesus to greatness without any self-consciousness, self-congratulation or even recognition.

I was recently seated at a dinner table with people to whom I had just been introduced and the talk turned, as it always does, to families. Their three fine sons were there and we were admiring them; and she said, "We have a daughter too," and she quickly got out her wallet and showed us a picture of a lovely young woman. "She is severely handicapped. She can't communicate; but we love her and we're proud of her too."

And I thought about that mother and her daughter, close to her heart every day for twenty-five years, and about Jesus' words that greatness is serving.

At the end of her letter, Emilie thanked Nancy—who made the simple suggestion that going to Rwanda was a call. Of course it was—the call of Jesus Christ to men and women, to each of us, to realize our full humanity, our highest potential, our greatness as children of God, by serving.

Gerald May is a physician who has written beautifully about these matters. In a recent book he is discussing the physical state of stability, the goal of the physician: to stabilize us. It's called homeostasis. May writes:

Love does not permit homeostasis to be the end of things. If we so choose, whatever stability we have can be the source of endless beginnings. Our equilibrium can be gestation rather than stagnation. Homeostasis can be the place where we wake up to our yearnings, however painful, and claim them as our own. We can choose to follow our desires. . . . We can say yes to the invitation of love and begin to open up and reach out again. Each time we say yes we upset our stability. We sacrifice our serenity. We risk our safety. We become vulnerable to being hurt. And creation shines more brightly. (*The Awakened Heart* [HarperSanFrancisco, 1991], 370]

Jesus said, "Whoever wants to be great among you must be your servant."

—September 25, 1994

ELEVEN

Why I Am a Presbyterian

"No one puts new wine into old wineskins."
Mark 2:22 (NRSV)

WHY I AM A PRESBYTERIAN. IT IS sometimes said that the trouble with most religion is that it is busy providing answers to questions nobody is asking. I am quite sure that few people lie awake asking, "Why is he a Presbyterian?"

And yet—it is an interesting and critical moment for religious denominations in this country. Are they anachronisms, phenomena which emerged out of a particular historic situation and which now need to fade away? Or are they of permanent value? Is there something about Presbyterianism, Methodism, Lutheranism that needs preserving and deserves celebrating?

For the record, I'm a Presbyterian because my parents were. I was baptized in a Presbyterian church, attended

79

Sunday School, was confirmed, participated in youth fellowship and church camp. Presbyterianism is almost as deeply a part of who I am as my name.

But I am also a Presbyterian because I chose to be. When I left the basic structures of life—family and community—I also left my church for a while and wandered around in the wilderness, trying to decide who I was and who I wanted to be. And I discovered what many of us discover in that particular wilderness, namely that while our family may not be the most wonderful family in the world, it is our family and there is much about it that is admirable. And so with my church; from the outside looking in, it appeared different, stronger, more attractive than it did from the inside looking out—not unlike Noah's Ark, I suppose, to which the church is often likened and about which someone quipped that the stench inside is sometimes so bad that leaving sounds like a good idea, except for the fact that there is a storm outside and a person could easily drown.

In any event, after a serious flirtation with another ecclesiastical tradition, and an even more serious consideration of the most politically correct option—the time being the 1960s—namely a complete rejection of institutional religion as hypocritical and oppressive, I came back to where I had started, reclaimed my tradition, or rather claimed it authentically for myself, and asked the Presbyterian Church if it would have me.

In June of 1963 I was home again, for the first time, now a minister of Word and Sacrament; and the symbol of that decision—my decision to be a Presbyterian and that of the Presbyterians to allow me in—is the two white strips of cloth we wear on Sunday. Not all Presbyterian ministers wear them, by the way. But Fourth Church clergy always have, and I always have. They are sometimes called "preaching bands," or "Geneva tabs." They are said to represent the two foundations of Calvinism—The Law and the Grace of God. I don't know about that. What they mean to me is Geneva, where this church, this tradition, my family—which I am grateful and proud to number my self among—began. Geneva tabs remind me weekly of who I am and of this unique religious tradition called Reformed/Presbyterian which I claim as my own.

And yet, even that—that personal loyalty to a particular religious tradition—is a bit of an anachronism, is it not?

Brand loyalty, denominational orientation, does not rank very high when people choose a church. Ask a group of Presbyterians anywhere why they are members of a particular congregation and they will say things like, "It's close; we like the music, the children's program, the preaching, the people, the building; my wife or husband or parents make me go." Almost no one says, "I belong because it's Presbyterian." The same is true for Methodists, United Church of Christ, and, to an extent, Episcopalians.

Interestingly, denominations originally served to preserve ethnic or national identity for immigrants to the new world. As national and ethnic identity receded, denominations in this culture took on a new function. In 1929 H. Richard Niebuhr wrote a classic study called "The Social Sources of Denominationalism" which observed that there was a religious social hierarchy. Vance Packard wrote about it in his famous 1959 book *The Status Seekers* [McKay, 1959]. He referred to "the long road from Pentecostal to Episcopal." Based on income, people might move from Pentecostal to Baptist to Methodist to Presbyterian to Episcopal, the top of the heap economically.

But even the social function of denominations is now gone. The old social hierarchy is gone. Wade Clark Roof and William McKinney are two sociologists who study religion. In their widely read *American Mainline Religions* [Rutgers University Press, 1987], they describe our numerical decline and then include a hilarious *Wall Street Journal* feature article written by Jack Cashill.

> My strategy is to consolidate the various name brands, even the strong, flagship brands like Southern Baptist, into one identifiable, Exxon-like entity. The target audience here is Mom, Dad, Butch and Sis—solid suburban Americans who want a little God in their life and a place to go before brunch. And after test-marketing various possibilities, I have decided on the name Middle American Christian Church, or MacChurch for ad purposes. (Jack Cashill, *Wall Street Journal*, 30 July 1985, in Roof and McKinney, 229)

Cashill, an advertising executive, created a marketing plan for revitalizing the major religious faiths. Judaism, he said, definitely needs a new product for baby boomers; for Roman Catholics a market-segmentation approach: "'RC Light' for liberals, 'RC Classic' for traditionalists, 'RC Free' for those interested in liberation theology." Protestantism presents special problems: Individual churches will have to understand that there is only so much theological shelf space, that product differentiation is not viable for go-as-you-please Protestants; thus the Middle American Christian Church or "MacChurch" (Jack Cashill, *Wall Street Journal*, 30 July 1985, in Roof and McKinney, 229).

Product differentiation is not very important. It never really was intended to be. The theological differences between Presbyterians, Methodists, Lutherans, United Church of Christ, Baptists are minimal. We differ in the way we go about being a church, but there are no substantive differences in our beliefs. The same is true between Protestants and Catholics. The fundamentals are the same. We believe in God the Creator, and Jesus Christ as God's incarnation, and the work of the Spirit in the world, and the Christian vocation to be faithful and to live in the love of Christ.

So, when someone says, "tell me what Presbyterians believe," the answer is the same things as Methodists or Baptists or Catholics believe: the Gospel of Jesus Christ. Our own new member statistics indicate that product differentiation is no longer very important at all. In the five months between June and October, we received 110 new members: only twenty-three, one in five, were Presbyterians.

What does differentiate between churches is the ethos, the style, the mission priorities, and the matter of authority—who has it and how it is exercised. And so bear with me as we think about who we are.

We began in the middle of the sixteenth century, about thirty years after Martin Luther challenged the authority of the Roman Church and started the Protestant Reformation. John Calvin was a French lawyer who was interested in Reformation thinking, was exiled from France, settled in Geneva, Switzerland, wrote one of the most important theological and political works ever produced, *The Institutes of the Christian Religion*, became a Reformed pastor, and was persuaded by the Geneva political powers to settle there and to organize the church and the city according to the new principles he had been writing about. So he did and the result was a new way of being a church.

Calvin imagined a church whose authority was not in its hierarchy but its people. That was a revolutionary idea, a dangerous and radical idea in the political arena. Calvin said that not only does the individual have the right to participate in the process by which authority is exercised, both ecclesiastical and civil; no authority has the right to coerce the individual's conscience. God alone is the Lord of the conscience.

And furthermore, said Calvin, the individual who has rights and authority needs to be educated, to be able to read and reason, and so it is one of the primary responsibilities of civil authority, not just wealthy families, to educate the young. And, he said, truth leads to goodness; religious faith is to be expressed, not just in personal morality and piety, but in responsible and compassionate and just political action.

And so there is a Presbyterian ethos, a style, a way of being a church. Authority here is not in the hierarchy, but the people who elect representatives called elders. A Presbyterian particular is to be very suspicious of authority which is not representative. A minister can't make many decisions without the session. We have no bishops and we get nervous when anyone starts acting like one. We call our highest officers moderator and clerk, not terribly exalted titles.

And this matter of conscience. The sons and daughters of John Calvin have been everywhere on the side of liberty in the political arena. It was an important moment for me when in freshman government I had to read John Calvin on the principles of liberty. John Knox, a disciple of Calvin, took Presbyterianism back to Scotland and fomented a revolution which resulted in freedom of religion and conscience. Presbyterians were here, on this continent, in 1640 and by the time of the American Revolution had strongly sided with the patriot cause. William Pitt, on the floor of Parliament, called the skirmish in the colonies "the Presbyterian revolt." The only clergy to sign the Declaration of Independence was one of ours, John Witherspoon, minister and president of the College of New Jersey. You will find the Presbyterian Church pressing for personal freedom all along the often controversial political spectrum. We were deeply involved in the civil rights movement; we are historically opposed to any government coercion of conscience; we are for the dignity and rights of individuals to determine their own destiny.

And education—the majority of the colleges in the colonies and post-colonial period were started by Presbyterians and other Reformed churches; and across the country, some sixty colleges and universities today are still related to the Presbyterian Church.

One of our very distinguished theologians, Edward Farley, says, "If we have a genius it is not so much some distinctive deposit of doctrine as it is a way of transcending our deposited traditions under the constant nagging pressure of the question of truth" ("The Presbyterian Heritage as Modernism," in *The Presbyterian Predicament*, ed. by Milton J. Coalter, et al. [Westminster/John Knox, 1990], 52).

Because we believe so passionately in the sovereignty of God and the human conscience, we believe that the question of truth is an open one and that we are called to seek the truth with our minds and hearts and spirits. We believe that science and academic inquiry are holy pursuits—never, never the enemy of religion.

One of the great moments in the history of this congregation, in fact, was when David Swing, one of its pastors in the years after the Civil War, was tried for heresy by the Presbytery of Chicago for saying that "Church confessions were not deposits of absolute truth but statements having a useful function for a specific time and situation." The Presbytery exonerated him. Our heritage includes:

- individual rights and responsibilities in church and world
- the pursuit of truth and the life of the mind
- commitment to education
- commitment to the life of faith in the world

I believe this is a precious and important inheritance and that the life of the world, the nation, the community, would be immeasurably poorer without them. You will not hear much about that kind of religion on television. How tragic if mindless piety, not open to new truth, were all the culture ever heard about Christianity.

Farley thinks, and I believe, that the phrase that best describes us is "critical modernism."

We accept science—scientific inquiry, not as the only arbiter of truth, but as a gift of God and a human responsibility.

We are not biblical literalists. We believe it is critically important to engage in historical analysis of the Bible. We shouldn't hide that or be ashamed of it. We should celebrate it and teach our children that the truth of Scripture is accessible to the human intellect when it is doing what it does best—challenge, probe, question.

And we are "modernists," a word often used as a criticism. We live in this world. Our hearts and minds and bodies belong to God, but we live in the 1990s; and frankly we are far more concerned about the future than we are about the past—the world we are giving to our children and grandchildren, than the world of our grandparents.

And I'm a Presbyterian because I choose to stand in a line of others who have faithfully witnessed to God's love and grace in Jesus Christ and the consequent social and political imperatives.

I'm a Presbyterian because of the witness of my church in the world. I am a member of our church's board of pensions. We met last week in California and while there visited a retirement facility for mission personnel at Duarte. We own the facility because retired missionaries don't have much of anything: no home, no equity, often no furniture and no savings. I was deeply touched.

I met and talked with a woman who with her husband had taught for forty years at the American University in Beirut, a very critical university started by her husband's great-grandfather, a Presbyterian missionary in the 1860s.

And I was hosted on our visit by Ralph and Florence Galloway, who worked for forty years in Central Africa—he, as a pastor and linguist who spent his life developing a written language for tribal people whose dialect was only spoken and who therefore had no way to communicate with the outside world; she, as a public health nurse, specializing in family planning and women's reproductive health issues. They were proud of their first refrigerator and a computer.

And I ate dinner with old friends, Dr. and Mrs. Norval Christy—he an eye surgeon, she his nurse and surgical assistant. At the Presbyterian hospital in Taxila, Pakistan, Dr. and Mrs.

Christy developed cataract surgery techniques that allowed their team of Pakistanis to do 150 cataract operations a day, every day. People from all over the world came to watch and learn. "What's going on in Taxila these days?" I asked. Dr. Christy doesn't talk much. "They do it now," he said. "Who?" I asked. "They do, my Pakistani doctors. I trained seven of them and they are expanding the clinic." "Christians," I asked. "Yes, all seven."

I'm a Presbyterian because I love this family and what it means and does. In Beirut, Pakistan, and Zaire; in great American churches like Nassau Presbyterian in Princeton, Fifth Avenue in New York, Peachtree in Atlanta, in Philadelphia, Pittsburgh, Cleveland, Denver, Dallas, Seattle, San Francisco, Chicago—large, faithful, robust, lively Presbyterian churches in the city; and in Decatur, Alton, and Springfield—more than eleven thousand congregations in the United States. And here in Chicago at 64th and Kimbark, First Presbyterian, and Second Church at Michigan and 20th; 130 congregations in and around the city, a new congregation in Hoffman Estates, a store front in Humbolt Park; the Center for Whole Life in Cabrini-Green [public-housing project], and children tutored and houses built and homeless fed, God's love expressed in the world by Presbyterian churches and individual Presbyterian Christians.

No one puts new wine in old wineskins, Jesus once said. It is surely the clearest thing he ever said. No tradition survives which does not always seek new ways to be expressed and celebrated.

T. S. Eliot wrote an essay about tradition once in which he said that tradition is not something you inherit; if you want tradition you must obtain it with great labor. You must obtain it with intellectual toil, existential engagement, contestation and interrogation (see Cornell West in Criterion, University of Chicago Divinity School, Spring/Summer, 1994).

There are many ways to be faithful. There are many ways to respond to Christ's call to discipleship. Presbyterianism is one, not the only one. But it is ours, yours and mine for a while: to enjoy, celebrate, and employ in the way we work out our own vocations. And, along with all the other unique church traditions, this one, I think, is to be appreciated and respected. It is a gift to us to be handed on to others, generation to generation.

—October 30, 1994

TWELVE

And Mercy Shall Follow Me

"Surely goodness and mercy shall follow me all the days of my life."

Psalm 23:6 (NRSV)

THE ARTICLE ON THE FRONT PAGE of the paper was deeply disturbing. I thought about it all day. A young man, fourteen years old, had shot and killed another young man, thirteen, who was standing outside his apartment in the Robert Taylor Homes. The victim was a lively, bright boy, supported and loved by his parents and strong extended family—aunts, uncles, cousins, grandparents. The boy on trial had no family, did not know who his father was. His mother did not even come to his trial. The court psychologist testified that he was passive and fatalistic. Now, sadly, this is not an unusual story to see on the front page of the newspaper. One teenager killing another. What I found chilling was that no one involved—

defense attorneys, social worker, psychologist—not even the
judge—could extract from the defendant anything resembling
remorse for the act of killing, or compassion for the victim and his
family. His guilt was not in question. He testified that he had shot
at the building because a gang superior told him to, gave him the
rifle to do it. He shot and killed a thirteen year old—an innocent
bystander. And during the trial, he listened intently but showed no
signs of remorse.

It is a kind of ultimate urban nightmare—an adolescent with
no feelings and an automatic weapon in his hand. In twenty years
or so he'll be out of prison, and unless the penal system instills in
him or elicits from him something like mercy or compassion, he
will, everybody knows, do it again. We have, the *New York Times*
editorialized not long ago, a "crisis of compassion" in the land.
We have adolescents with no capacity to feel pity. And we have
politicians using "bleeding heart, do-gooder" as an insult, as if
caring too much was a sign of weakness, as if it were a bad idea
to be merciful.

In his best-selling collection of stories, *The Book of Virtues* [Simon
& Schuster, 1993], William Bennett comments, "Compassion is a
virtue that takes seriously the reality of other persons, their inner
lives, their emotions, as well as their external circumstances. . . .
Compassion thus comes close to the very heart of moral awareness
. . ." (p. 106). And one of the most famous lines of Shakespeare is
spoken by Portia, in *The Merchant of Venice*, about mercy.

> [Mercy] is twice blest;
> It blesseth him that gives and him that takes . . . :
> It is enthroned in the hearts of kings,
> It is an attribute [of] God himself,
> And earthly power doth then show likest God's,
>   When mercy seasons justice.

Perhaps earthly power is like God's power when mercy seasons
justice. But no one I know won an election recently talking like
that—about mercy and compassion. What garners votes these days
is capital punishment, reductions in health care and education to
our children, reducing benefits to immigrants. The simple fact is
that we seem to be convinced that compassion and economic reality

are mutually exclusive. We have become persuaded that we cannot afford mercy.

And yet it is at the very heart of our religious tradition—at the heart of what the tradition means by the word "God."

When the Hebrew people were wandering around in the wilderness of Sinai, their religious worship focused on the Ark of the Covenant. When they made camp, they erected a tent around the ark called the tabernacle. The theological idea was radical. It was that God traveled with the people: God is not confined to a particular temple or sacred spot, but lived with the people wherever they were. In the first lesson this morning, we heard a description of one of the features of the Ark, something called the Mercy seat, a "slab of specifically refined gold on top of the Ark" (*Interpreter's Dictionary of the Bible*); "The most sacred object in the most holy place [the mercy seat] was the throne of Yahweh" (*Interpreter's Bible*). "I will meet you there"—at the mercy seat— God says in Exodus 25.

The interesting thing about it is the name, "mercy seat." Where did that come from, all the way back there on the edge of history? Why not judgment seat? Or anger seat? Or jealousy seat? Or power seat? Why mercy—in a time when mercy, compassion, and kindness were not common attributes one associated with God? Primitive religion usually focuses on the power or mystery of the divine, not mercy. What is happening, of course, is the earliest appearance of a magnificent idea. It is the basic nature of God to be merciful. This primitive symbol of the mercy seat is saying that above and beyond all else God is—God is merciful.

From that original amazing grace came the further genius of the Judeo-Christian tradition. The needy, the weak, and the vulnerable always get special mercy. God is particularly attentive to the poor and oppressed. And there is a political and social ethic which follows. The people, the nation, will be held accountable for the degree of mercy it shows to the weakest and smallest and most vulnerable: the aged, orphans, widows, sick and poor. Individuals, likewise, are accountable not for verbal affirmations of piety. Love for God translates into merciful action towards your fellow human beings.

The most eloquent expression of this radical idea was written by the prophet Micah: "With what shall I come before the Lord?

Burnt offerings, calves, thousands of rams, rivers of oil? He has told you what is good, what the Lord requires: do justice, love kindness [mercy], walk humbly with God." Jesus expressed that ancient tradition of God's mercy and of mercy as the basis of common morality.

Most human behavior is based on reciprocity. You do this for me, and I will do this back to you. But the radical ethic of Jesus was not based on reciprocity. When someone strikes you, don't respond in kind. Everybody does that. Turn the other cheek, he said. Everybody hates their enemies. You must do good to those who hate you. Even love. It's no great moral accomplishment to love people who love you. Normally, human behavior is reactive: Someone is surly—be surly back. Someone shoves you out of place when you're waiting in line—shove back. When on the expressway someone tailgates me, then impatiently pulls out and cuts in front too close, I confess, everything in me wants to respond in kind, and sometimes I do. Insult me and I'll insult you. Hit me and I'll hit you harder. It's the story of human history, is it not?

The effect, of course, is to give enormous power to the other person, the one who is acting so badly. If your behavior is only responsive and reactive, your ethical mentor is precisely the one who is treating you so unethically. The result is often tragedy. Revenge, retribution carried out by one nation against another, by society against the individual, or by one person on another person, is not moral, according to Jesus. It's not even smart. It does not discourage bad behavior. No one believes that capital punishment actually has anything to do with the crime rate. What it has to do with is reciprocal morality—revenge—the momentary intoxication of getting even.

Jesus subverted that entire way of thinking and the theology behind it. He challenged and undercut the way his own people thought and acted. They didn't like it at all, nor do we.

What is the source of moral behavior, then, if it is not reaction, response, revenge? It was one of the simplest and most powerful things he ever said: "Be merciful, just as your Father is merciful." It is a challenging assignment these days.

The lead editorial in the January 1 *New York Times*, "The Quality of Mercy in 1995," commented: "A new brand of hard-talking officeholders and social engineers has created a compassion crisis in American political life. How else to explain the withdrawal of all aid from an infant whose mother does not meet Congressionally mandated rules as to work and sexual behavior?" And then this— "American voters, to be sure, want more efficient social spending and return to bedrock values of family and community, but one of those values is compassion."

The *Chicago Tribune* on Tuesday included an editorial, "More Children Sink into Poverty," which documented the increasing dilemma of the working poor. The number of American children living in poverty increased by one million to six million, or 26 percent of all children, between 1987 and 1992. The editorial pointed to a "20-year trend of economic bifurcation, hour-glass shaped growth of the lowest and highest income brackets, with the largest toll on poor children."

There are, I think, a lot of rational, commonsense and non-political reasons for rethinking the role of government in helping the disadvantaged and providing for children. But we do know that the most cost-effective move we can make is to provide a better chance for children. Someone said on *The Today Show* this week that the second-best dollar we can spend is on education for our children. The best dollar is on preschool and day care so that the children are ready to learn when they go to school. I think there is a logical case to be made for reforming welfare in a way that values family integrity, rewards hard work, and supports it with accessible employment, health care, and transportation. Those issues must continue to receive the best intelligence and creativity we can muster and it is, I believe, our calling—yours and mine— to add to the very important public debate the wisdom of our religious tradition that holds up mercy as the primary moral value.

But this is not finally about sociology or politics. It is about faith and faithfulness. It is about God and living in a way that honors God.

The quintessential story about mercy, of course, is the parable of the Good Samaritan. It is a story of a man from Samaria, who happens upon another man lying in the ditch beside the road, beaten and bleeding. Two important religious officials have already passed by, seeing him and deciding to ignore him. The

hero of the story, the Samaritan, stops, binds up his wounds, trans-
ports him to shelter, and pays for his care. The interesting thing
about that parable is that it is an answer to a theological, spiritual,
deeply personal question. "What must I do to inherit eternal life?"
someone had asked him—not, "What is appropriate social or political behavior?" The story originally had to do with the relative
health of an individual's soul. "How can I save my soul?" was the
real question. And the answer was, "If you will start to reflect in
your life the merciful love God has for you, you will find that God
is saving your soul."

This is not about social policy. It is about how to live faithfully,
how to follow Jesus. He said if you feel another's pain and minister to it, you will be living the kind of life God gives you to live,
a life rich in meaning and purpose and value.

That's a conclusion also reached by Robert Wuthnow, a sociol-
ogist at Princeton, who has done an important study, *Acts of
Compassion: Caring for Others and Helping Ourselves* [Princeton
University Press, 1991]. The study inquired into the kinds of volunteer service activities we are doing and what we get out of it.
Wuthnow observes: "Volunteers are not naive. They do not
believe, as some of their critics suggest, that acts of compassion
toward needy individuals will actually solve society's problems.
No. Volunteer work will save us because it implies hope" (p. 233).

I read a sweet little story about mercy and how close it is to the
heart of God and the idea of God's kingdom on earth, a kingdom
always closest to our children. It is in a book by Christopher
deVinck, *The Power of the Powerless* [Doubleday, 1988].

> One spring afternoon my five-year-old son, David, and I were
> planting raspberry bushes along the side of the garage. A
> neighbor joined us for a few moments. David pointed to the
> ground. "Look Daddy! What's that?" I stopped talking with my
> neighbor and looked down.
>
> "A beetle," I said.
>
> David was impressed and pleased with the discovery of this
> fancy, colorful creature. My neighbor lifted his foot and stepped

on the insect, giving his shoe an after-twist in the dirt. "That ought to do it," he laughed.

David looked up at me, waiting for an explanation, a reason. . . .

That night, just before I turned off the light in his bedroom, David whispered, "I liked that beetle, Daddy."

"I did too," I whispered back.

DeVinck concludes the story by saying, "We have the power to choose . . . the power to choose how we will respond to everything that crosses our path from beetles to human beings" (qtd. in "Birthing Compassion," Sue Monk Kidd, *Weavings*, November/December 1990, 18).

Citizens of a modern American city know better than anyone that the world can be a cruel, unfeeling place. But the tradition we bear, the religion we claim as our own, is based on the faith that into the world came the Creator to sit on something the people of God called a mercy seat. We will not, in fact, be dealt with according to our sins, as the psalmist promised (Psalm 103), but by God's steadfast and merciful love. That's an astonishing idea. Our relationship with God is based not on God's judging our moral purity, but God's mercy which knows us and loves us and is kind to us. Somehow those people came to understand that among all the attributes of God—power, majesty, mystery, omnipotence, righteousness, holiness, perfection, purity—the one that most thoroughly expressed the essence of God was mercy.

Later, one of their poets wrote a beautiful hymn about that God.

The Lord is my shepherd, I shall not want . . .
You prepare a table before me . . .
You anoint my head . . .
My cup overflows . . .
Surely goodness and mercy shall follow me
All the days of my life . . .

Later still, Jesus of Nazareth lived out the mercy of God, welcoming all to him, particularly those who were poor, needy, outcast, living a parable of God's mercy. "Be merciful," he told his friends, "as God is merciful."

The world needs that as never before. Our country needs a church strong enough to show what that means, to advocate and argue for mercy publicly and then honest enough to live it out—in our corporate life.

The world needs us, individual friends of Jesus sure enough of themselves to risk being called bleeding hearts; so sure of his mercy that one day we will be judged, not according to our mistakes and failures, but by a God whose essence is mercy; by a God whose justice is tempered by mercy; people so in love with that God that "bleeding heart" starts to feel like a badge of honor and not an insult—something to be proud of; humbly and faithfully merciful people who know and trust and bank their lives on the promise that mercy will follow us all the days of our lives.

—*February 19, 1995*